BRIGHT

LONG DAYS JOURNEY INTO NIGHT
BY
EUGENE O'NEILL

Intelligent Education

INFLUENCE PUBLISHERS

Nashville, Tennessee

BRIGHT NOTES: Long Days Journey into Night
www.BrightNotes.com

No part of this publication may be used or reproduced in any manner whatsoever without written permission, except in the case of brief quotations in critical articles and reviews. For permissions, contact Influence Publishers http://www.influencepublishers.com.

ISBN: 978-1-645421-18-4 (Paperback)
ISBN: 978-1-645421-19-1 (eBook)

Published in accordance with the U.S. Copyright Office Orphan Works and Mass Digitization report of the register of copyrights, June 2015.

Originally published by Monarch Press.
Paul W. Gannon, 1965
2020 Edition published by Influence Publishers.

Interior design by Lapiz Digital Services. Cover Design by Thinkpen Designs.

Printed in the United States of America.

Library of Congress Cataloging-in-Publication Data forthcoming.
Names: Intelligent Education
Title: BRIGHT NOTES: Long Days Journey into Night
Subject: STU004000 STUDY AIDS / Book Notes

CONTENTS

EUGENE O'NEILL

INTRODUCTION

. . . .

EARLY LIFE

Eugene O'Neill was born in a Broadway hotel on October 16, 1888. His father was a popular actor of romantic melodrama and Eugene's first seven years were spent in the larger towns all over the United States. The success of the *Count of Monte Cristo*, in which his father played the lead, kept the family engaged in almost continuous road tours. From the age of seven to thirteen he attended boarding schools. In 1902 he was sent to Betts Academy at Stamford and the autumn after his graduation he entered Princeton. Although his parents were Catholic, and he had been in and out of parochial schools from an early age, by the time he entered Princeton he had left the Church and never returned to it.

DISCONTENT WITH COLLEGE

In June of 1903 he was dismissed from Princeton, supposedly for throwing a beer bottle through a window of President Wilson's house. He could have returned the following year, but he had become bored with college and left to become a secretary in a New York mail-order house, the first in a long series of jobs he held before settling down to write.

YEARS OF WANDERING

In 1909 he married Kathleen Jenkins, a union that ended in divorce in 1912. In the same year he went on a gold-prospecting trip to Honduras. He had been reading Jack London, Kipling and Conrad, and we can see in the many journeys of his youth a desire to lead the rugged life of adventure that those writers took as their central **theme**. In 1910 he shipped on a Norwegian barque for Buenos Aires where he worked at some odds jobs, but ended up, in his own words, "a bum on the docks." In 1911, after a trip to Africa on a cattle steamer, he returned to New York where he lived at "Jimmy the Priest's," a waterfront dive which provided the setting for the first act of *Anna Christie*. After a last voyage to England he found himself on a train to New Orleans following a wild party. His father was playing there in the perennially popular Monte Cristo. He refused to give his son a handout, but did give him a part in the play. At the close of the season the O'Neills returned to their summer home in New London, Connecticut, where Eugene worked as a cub reporter on the Telegraph.

HIS DESIRE TO WRITE

In December of 1912 O'Neill entered a tuberculosis sanatorium. Weakened by years of irregular living, his health had broken down. During his fifteen month convalescence he first felt the urge to write. When he left the sanatorium he was a man with a purpose. To rebuild his health he disciplined himself to a life of exercise and hard work. In the next sixteen months he wrote eleven one-act plays, two long plays, and some poetry. He read omnivorously, in his own words "the Greeks and Elizabethans-practically all the classics - and of course all the moderns."

FIRST PLAYS

In the fall of 1914 he went to Harvard to take Professor George Baker's famous course in playwriting. In the same year his father financed the publication of his first book, *Thirst and Other One-act Plays*. Several plays in Thirst take men against the sea as their **theme**. O'Neill's classic statement of his **theme** is in the so-called Glencairn group, a sequence of one-act plays dealing with the tramp steamer Glencairn. The group consists of *The Moon of the Caribbees*, *Bound East for Cardiff*, *The Long Voyage Home* and *In the Zone*. In these plays man is shown in conflict with nature, which is indifferent to his suffering and inevitable doom. In his early naturalism O'Neill was deeply indebted to Jack London.

FIRST SUCCESS

In 1916 the Provincetown Players put on *Bound East for Cardiff*. It was O'Neill's first play to be acted. The Players were a group of Greenwich Village journalists, writers and painters who were interested in rejuvenating the American theater. In 1917-18 he had three plays published in Smart Set, a magazine of protest against the self-satisfied middle class, whose editors, H. L. Mencken and George Jean Nathan, were already known as literary critics. The production of *Beyond the Horizon* in 1920 brought O'Neill his first Pulitzer Prize, and from then until his death no one seriously questioned that he was the leading American playwright of his generation. In 1918 he had married Agnes Boulton Burton, and now, riding the wave of success, he had great faith in the future. However, he resolved he would never sell out to success. His father had felt that the temptation of easy money to be had from a play such as *Monte Cristo* had ruined his chances of becoming a fine actor. O'Neill resolved he would remain true to his dream and work to express the truth he had in him.

DISILLUSIONMENT

In spite of his remarkable success, O'Neill was convinced that bad fortune was hounding him. Throughout his life, except for brief periods, he had the feeling that man is at the mercy of mysterious forces beyond his control. He began to look back with nostalgia upon his seafaring days, and longed to be on the move again.

FINANCIAL SUCCESS

In the fall of 1920 *The Emperor Jones* was staged in London, Paris, Berlin, Tokyo and Buenos Aires, laying the foundation for O'Neill's international reputation. One year later *Anna Christie* opened in New York and brought him his second Pulitzer Prize. In 1922 *The Hairy Ape* was a success. It dramatized the idea that man has lost his old harmony with nature and is out of place in the modern, technological world. Late in 1922 O'Neill was making $850 a week in royalties. He bought a farm at Ridgefield, Connecticut, and settled down to live in landed elegance as his father had always desired to do.

HIS PESSIMISM

However, O'Neill could not settle down and two years later he was living in Bermuda and working on the idea for *Mourning Becomes Electra.* His idea of man at the mercy of mysterious forces had broadened through his reading of Freud, a German psychologist (1856-1939), Nietzsche, a German ethical writer who detested Christianity (1844-19000), and Schopenhauer, a German philosopher of the romantic period (1788-1860). From Freud he took the idea of man trapped by his unconscious sexual desires. Schopenhauer's pessimistic philosophy reinforced the naturalistic determinism that had been fostered by his reading of London and Conrad, and his own erratic life. From Nietzsche he took a joyous acceptance of despair as the only sane attitude for a man faced with an indifferent universe.

HONORED FOR HIS WORK

In 1926 he received the degree of Doctor of Literature from Yale University. Although at the height of his career, his personal life was a shambles. The following year he left his wife and two children to court Carlotta Monterey, the actress who had starred in *The Hairy Ape.* In 1928 *Strange Interlude* won a third Pulitzer Prize for him. Eugene and Carlotta took a whirlwind trip around the world and settled in a French chateau where he finished *Mourning Becomes Electra.* The play was presented in New York in October of 1931 and was immediately hailed as his masterpiece. Joseph Wood Krutch wrote that "it may turn out to be the only permanent contribution yet made by the twentieth century to dramatic literature."

AWARDED NOBEL PRIZE

From 1932 to 1936 O'Neill lived on an island off the coast of Georgia. The only successful play he wrote during this period was Ah, Wilderness!, the only comedy he ever composed. The play ran for 289 performances and brought O'Neill $75,000. In November of 1936 he moved to Oregon with plans to write a cycle of plays designed to tell the story of the United States from the early 1700s. In the same month he became the first American playwright to receive the Nobel Prize.

HIS LAST WORK

During the latter part of his life only a few O'Neill plays were produced. In 1941 he completed the autobiographical *Long Day's Journey Into Night* which was first staged in 1956, three years after his death. It won his fourth Pulitzer Prize. His vision of life had not changed and the characters are unable to control the dark forces that shape their destinies. *The Iceman Cometh* was staged in 1946. It was an enormous success, but the play is uncompromisingly nihilistic in its philosophy. He suggests that man's urge toward the unattainable is his only justification, but what the unattainable is he can never know. O'Neill died in 1953 at the age of sixty-five. No one doubted that he was the greatest playwright America had produced.

LONG DAY'S JOURNEY INTO NIGHT

INTRODUCTION

The best introduction to this play was written by O'Neill himself. In dedicating the original manuscript to his wife, he said her love gave him the "faith in love" necessary to write this play, to "write it with deep pity and understanding and forgiveness for all the four haunted Tyrones." Each word of the dedication is fraught with meaning, but for our purpose the most important words are "faith in love," and "haunted Tyrones."

Certainly it was O'Neill's new-found "faith in love" that made possible his pity, understanding, and forgiveness. Critics, commentators, and psychologists have alluded to his "unhappy and insecure childhood" in attempting to account for his predilection for tragedy; perhaps at last he did finally find love, happiness, and security. Brooks Atkinson commented thus on *Long Day's Journey*: "The pity, the understanding and the forgiveness that spread through the last act are like a kind of sorrowful benediction and bring a relentless drama to a magnificent conclusion." (See "O'Neill's Journey," *New York Times* (November 18, 1956, II, 1.)

The use of the adjective "haunted" in the dedication stresses the importance of the supernatural, the spiritual, the unknown. This concern with a Force or power over which man has no control is echoed in the mother's comment, "None of us can help the things life has done to us." In this play we see that although O'Neill was unable to explain Life, he was able to accept what Life offered. Lionel Trilling once wrote, "To affirm that life exists and is somehow good - this, then, became O'Neill's quasi-religious poetic function...." (See "Eugene O'Neill," *The New Republic,* 88 (September 23, 1936) 179).

Perhaps like Schopenhauer (German philosopher, 1788-1860) O'Neill would say, "If our life were endless and painless it would probably occur to no one why the world exists."

THE AUTOBIOGRAPHICAL ELEMENTS

To show that *Long Day's Journey Into Night* is autobiographical is not necessary-O'Neill's dedication and the fact that he originally stipulated that it not be published until twenty-five years after his death prove its authenticity as a page from the author's life. (It is interesting to note that after his death, his wife gave permission to have it published, but Random House, which held the manuscript, felt duty-bound not to publish it. The manuscript was then given to Yale University which subsequently published it.) Our concern in this section is with the facts of O'Neill's life as they were in August 1912, the date of the play, and what had happened immediately prior to that time.

In December of 1911, O'Neill was forced to go through with a rather sordid **episode** at a brothel in order to give his first wife grounds for divorce. (In New York State the only grounds for divorce is adultery.) At the request of her lawyer, arrangements were made so that "official witnesses" could testify to his infidelity. Being forced to submit to such a sham was undoubtedly humiliating. Prior to this "**episode**" O'Neill had been on an extended binge, but soon after, he found himself connected with his father's acting company (to the dismay of both).

Very early in 1912, O'Neill returned to New York and resumed his attempt to drink and forget. His mother's drug addiction had grown worse and James O'Neill, Sr., had been forced to send her to a sanitarium near Denver. To top everything off, his roommate at the dive where he had holed-up committed suicide - and O'Neill attempted to follow suit. How sincere this attempt was we are not sure - but in *Long Day's Journey* Edmund [O'Neill] does say he is a "little in love with death.") By July, he and his father had reached a kind of understanding, and O'Neill agreed to spend the summer in New London. Using his father's influence to get the job, he went to work as a reporter for the *New London Telegraph*.

These are the facts as we know them. How true his portraits of the individual members of the family were, we will discuss later. In this play the characters, the setting, the references to the past, and the family relationships are, for the most part, "true to life." The one notable exception is the lack of any mention of O'Neill's first wife or any allusion to his marriage. Whether he considered the incident too unimportant or too painful, whether he wished to ignore her or forget her, we will never know. However, this is the only significant event or person figuring in O'Neill's life up to this time that is omitted.

Although the play is autobiographical it would be wrong to assume that the play is an accurate accounting of the events of a single day. *Long Day's Journey* is a confession, a revelation, a baring of O'Neill's soul, but it is also a work of art and not simply a verbatim account of everyday incidents. Consequently, events before and after the fact are included and others are invented. (For instance, O'Neill did not actually learn he had tuberculosis until very late in the fall of 1912.) A writer very often chooses, alters, and arranges his material so that the "truth" he presents is more "real" than the events to which he may allude.

THE SIGNIFICANCE OF THE TITLE

O'Neill was much concerned with the **connotations** of particular words and the importance of particular ideas. His titles were not simply "tacked on" to the manuscripts but must be considered as integral parts. Like other dramatists, O'Neill used the title to direct the audience's attention to particular ideas or important concerns. And this title, *Long Day's Journey Into Night,* like the play, seems to be O'Neill's attempt to summarize, complete, and conclude his life's work as a dramatist.

A long day would not only connote that the day seemed long but would also indicate that much happened. A journey indicates travel or movement from one place to another - in this instance it is symbolically from hope (day) into despair (night). And night refers not only to the opposite of day but also in a spiritual sense to ignorance, gloom, and painful confusion (such as the dark night of the soul). But O'Neill goes one step further than these rather obvious meanings.

The word day is commonly used to designate a twenty-four hour period, but it is also used to mark any particularly significant period. The long day for O'Neill refers to the past, to what has gone before, to the events which have brought him to his "moment of truth." The journey was for O'Neill his attempt to find himself and then to accept what he found. The night (the darkness, despair, and confusion) having been endured and accepted, and thus overcome, the brightness of a new day (life, man's existence) can be appreciated. O'Neill's *Journey* was physical, mental, moral, and spiritual and at its conclusion he found contentment in forgiveness (note the play's introduction).

Because O'Neill intended that this play be published posthumously, we might well consider it his **epitaph**, the capstone of his work. Many of his early plays were concerned with journeys, with man's attempt to find something or himself -*Bound East for Cardiff*, *The Long Voyage Home*, *Beyond the Horizon*, *The Fountain*. Winifred L. Dusenbury commented, "O'Neill's constant **theme** has been that of man's search for something outside himself to which he can belong, and since many of his characters do not succeed in attaining a mystical union or an ideal state of belonging, they succumb to loneliness." (See *The **Theme** of Loneliness in Modern American Drama*, University of Florida Press, 1960, p. 197.) And John Gassner in "The Nature of O'Neill's Achievement: a Summary and Appraisal" said, "His work reveals a keen sense of loss of connections - of connections with God, nature, society, family, father." (See *O'Neill-a Collection of Critical Essays*, Prentice-Hall, 1964, p. 168.)

It is in this play that O'Neill finds himself and, finally, belongs. In an interview with Seymour Peck, O'Neill's wife (Carlotta Monterey) commented thus on the importance that this play had for him: "When he started *Long Day's Journey,* it was a most strange experience to watch that man begin tortured every day by his own writing.... I think he felt freer when he got it out of his system. It was his way of making peace with his family - and himself." (See "A Talk with Mrs. O'Neill," *New York Times*, November 4, 1956.)

O'NEILL AND THE GREEK TRADITION

There can be little doubt of the tremendous influence that the tradition of the Greek theatre had on the work of Eugene O'Neill. As a young man he had read many of the classical dramatists and was evidently profoundly moved by the breadth and depth of their vision and the intensity of their passions. (Some of the senior O'Neill's love of the Greek drama was also transferred to the eldest son, Eugene O'Neill, Jr., who became a Greek scholar.) In *Mourning Becomes Electra* O'Neill rendered a modern version of Sophocles' *Electra;* in other plays the author's vision, philosophy, and concerns reflect the Greek influence.

O'Neill often referred to his concern with tragedy and the tragic. During an interview in 1922, he said, "... tragedy, I think, has the meaning the Greeks gave it. To them it gave exaltation, an urge toward life and more life. It raised them to deeper spiritual understanding and released them from the petty greeds of everyday existence...." (See "The Extraordinary Story of Eugene O'Neill" in *The American Magazine*, November 1922, p. 142.) O'Neill was at the same time also answering the critics who called his plays "sordid," "depressing," and "pessimistic" for they seemed unwilling to accept O'Neill and his point of view. In a letter to the *New York Tribune* on February 13, 1921, he had written, "To me the tragic alone has that significant beauty which is truth. It is the meaning of life - and the hope. The noblest is eternally the most tragic."

The more perceptive critics soon began to recognize this classical influence and to comment on it. Barrett H. Clark wrote of O'Neill turning to "... Greek tragedy for a medium through which he might express dramatically another aspect of one of the problems of modern life." (See "Aeschylus and O'Neill" in *The English Journal*, XXI, No. 9 (November 1932) 701.) Arthur

Hobson Quinn quoted a letter from O'Neill which stated that he wanted "to see the transfiguring nobility of tragedy, in as near the Greek sense as one can grasp it, in seemingly the most ignoble, debased lives." And O'Neill's own life seemed to prepare him to write tragedies. Frederic I. Carpenter observed, "The playwright became the tragic agonist, and his life a drama more violently theatrical than that of any of his fictional heroes." (See *Eugene O'Neill*, Twayne Publications, June, 1964, p. 18.)

In *Long Day's Journey Into Night*, O'Neill observes the unities of time, place, and action. (Aristotle's *Poetics* specifically demanded unity of action and its confinement to a single day.) Also, the tremendous emotional impact which this play has on the audience acts like the catharsis of the Greek drama - the purging of the emotions through the arousal of pity and terror. And finally, the rapidity with which the play is brought to a conclusion (the **denouement** - the final unraveling or solution of the plot of the play) is in the best tradition of the Greek drama.

A number of commentators have written about the classical elements in this play. Tom F. Driver wrote, "... Greek tragedy tended to obliterate the future. In *Oedipus Rex* [A Greek Tragedy by Sophocles] we see a formal handling of time very similar to *Long Day's Journey Into Night*.... And when Mary Tyrone, holding her wedding dress, closes the long day's journey by saying, 'We were happy - for a time,' O'Neill might say with Sophocles, 'Count no man happy until he is dead.'" (See "On the Late Plays of Eugene O'Neill," *Tulane Drama Review*, III, No. 2. (December 1958) 11-12.)

O'NEILL'S SETTING FOR THE PLAY

Since the stage setting for the play is the living room of the Tyrone's summer home, we are correct in assuming that O'Neill basically recreated the family living room in New London, Conn. The room is comfortably but unpretentiously furnished and is quite ordinary in every way. Only two details are worthy of mention - the listing of books in the two bookcases and the two double doorways leading out of the room.

The small bookcase contains novels by Balzac, Zola and Stendhal, works by Schopenhauer, Nietzsche and Marx, plays by Ibsen, Shaw and Strindberg, poetry by Swinburne, Wilde and Dowson. The larger bookcase contains three sets of Shakespeare, historical works and miscellaneous volumes of old plays and poetry. In the last act the father and son discuss the relative merits of various authors and we learn that the small bookcase contains the works which influenced O'Neill and his thinking and the larger bookcase contains volumes appropriate to the father and his concerns and ideas.

The care with which O'Neill noted the names of the books underlines the importance he attached to them. Since he had little formal education beyond prep school, O'Neill often commented on the great influence certain writers and certain works had on him. In his application for admission into Professor Baker's drama course, he noted that he had read "all the modern plays ... and many books on the subject of the Drama." And in his comments after being awarded the Nobel Prize for Literature he proclaimed his debt to Strindberg (Swedish dramatist, 1949-1912) and Nietzsche (German philosopher, 1844-1900). O'Neill never hesitated to acclaim those who influenced him or to imitate those who inspired him.

As the play progresses we see that the father is much concerned with the past and that the contrast in the literary tastes of the two thus reflects the conflict in their ideas and attitudes. The duplicate sets of Shakespeare not only emphasize the value that Tyrone places on these works but also indicates his belief that Shakespeare is the "be-all and end-all" of literature to the exclusion of anything which is new or different. The historical works and volumes of old plays and poetry reflect the same thinking. Because a considerable part of the play concerns the conflict between Edmund (O'Neill) and his father, the books which have influenced each are tangible manifestations of the conflict and at least partially account for it. (Certainly each man is influenced by what he reads even as he may be influenced by what he fails to read.)

More obviously important than the bookcases are the two double doorways which lead into the living room. O'Neill notes that one opens into a front parlor which is rarely used and the other opens into a dark, windowless back parlor which acts a passageway to the dining room. These doorways are, of course, necessary for stage entrances and exists. But more important is their significance for O'Neill and the audience.

Because most entrances are made from the dark back parlor, the characters are shown symbolically and actually moving from darkness into light. Their conversations in the living room reveal much about themselves and about each other-but always behind them is the darkness and unhappiness of the past. For a few moments they come into the light and realize the truth about themselves and each other-but very soon they again attempt to hide.

The rarely-used front parlor seems to symbolize the "might-have-been" or the happiness of the past. During the play the only person who uses the parlor is the mother - and this use occurs near the end of the play. When she comes back into the living room, she has completely lost contact with reality and imagines herself as a young girl again. If the back parlor represents the things of the past they are trying to forget, perhaps the front parlor represents the things of the past they are trying to remember.

The front parlor, which is not shown, also in some way parallels Strindberg's *A Dream Play* which revolves around the secret of a locked door. (In his play Strindberg seems to say we should let life go by like a dream-to live it but not to judge it or attempt to explain it.) Both O'Neill and Strindberg were concerned with the past, with the agony of existence, and with man's struggle for self-realization. In the Provincetown playbill of January 3, 1924, for the presentation of *The Spook Sonata*, O'Neill wrote, "Strindberg remains . . . the greatest interpreter in the theatre . . . of our lives today. . . . All that is enduring in what we loosely call "Expressionism'-all that is artistically valid and sound theatre-can be clearly traced back through Wedkind to Strindberg's *A Dream Play.* . . ."

LONG DAY'S JOURNEY INTO NIGHT

ACT I

. . . .

As the scene opens Tyrone and Mary enter the living room from the back parlor. James Tyrone has his arm about her waist as he compliments her on the twenty pounds she has gained. Mary replies that if she is not careful she'll get too fat and teases him about the enormous breakfast he just ate.

Comment

The setting is the living room of James Tyrone's summer home on a morning in August 1912. Before a word is spoken the audience gains certain impressions about Mary and James Tyrone. O'Neill's description of them, their manner of entrance, and their few words at the beginning of this scene, all contribute to the over-all effect which the play will or should have on the audience.

O'Neill describes Mary as being fifty-four, with a young, graceful figure, a pale but once-attractive, Irish face, and thick pure white hair. She is extremely nervous and her once beautiful hands are never still. Her dress and hair are attractively styled and her voice is soft. But her most appealing quality is the simple, unaffected charm of a "shy convent-girl youthfulness she has never lost -an innate unworldly innocence." The description which we are given is so completely and thoughtfully wrought that each aspect of it should be examined carefully. Having been described as an attractive middle-aged woman we would perhaps conclude that Mary had endured few hardships during her life-physical, mental, or financial. Her demeanor, speech, and dress are all appropriate to a woman who has a successful husband and who has, therefore, had the time and money necessary to enjoy the "finer things in life." But there is a disconcerting note.

Mary's extreme nervousness and pale face belie the healthy figure. And when James tells her she's "a fine armful now," because of the twenty pounds she's gained, we realize she must have been ill. O'Neill calls attention to her hands and notes that "one avoids looking at them, the more so because one is conscious she is sensitive about their appearance and humiliated by her inability to control their nervousness which draws attention to them." Again and again throughout the play attention is called to the hands since Mary's inability to "control" their shaking is not only a symbolic but also a physical manifestation of her inability to control what she does and why she does it. More about this later.

Throughout the play attention is also called to the "convent-girl" quality of the mother. This quality of "unworldly innocence" is perhaps attractive, but rather out-of-place; endearing, and at the same time ironic; appealing, but nonetheless unrealistic for a wife and mother. As the play develops we begin to realize that

Mary's concern with the "might-have-been" seems to be in many ways both directly and indirectly responsible for the present plight of the whole family.

Because *Long Day's Journey* is autobiographical we had best comment briefly about the physical description of Mary which O'Neill here gives us. According to biographers who interviewed those who knew the O'Neill family at this time, the description of Mary Tyrone closely duplicates their recollections of Mary Ellen Quinlan O'Neill, Eugene O'Neill's mother. The adjectives used to describe her are perhaps most significant since they reveal the "idealized" way in which the author "saw" his mother: graceful figure, a once pretty face, sensitive lips, pure white hair, once beautiful hands, soft and attractive voice, simple, unaffected charm.

James Tyrone is sixty-five but looks ten years younger; he is remarkably good looking with the "air" of an actor about him. His clothes are shabby and threadbare-he is dressed for gardening and doesn't care how he looks. He radiates health and self-assurance. A little later we learn he is at times inclined toward a sentimental melancholy and rare flashes of intuitive sensibility.

The fact that James is sixty-five but looks ten years younger would indicate that the years had been good to him and his way of life had agreed with him. As a popular actor, "a matinee idol," he evidently enjoyed life on and off the stage. Because he has been successful, his pride in himself and what he has done is evident in his speech and bearing. But O'Neill notes that he is by nature and preference a simple, unpretentious man. The description of James Tyrone's clothes prepare us somewhat for a point the author is going to comment on throughout the play - the father's inclination towards stinginess.

Again alluding to the autobiographical element, the description of the father is not as "glowing" as that of the mother. No derogatory comments are made, but the description is somewhat tentative and qualified. The author shows a grudging respect for the father, James Tyrone, the same that he showed for his father, James O'Neill. Another indication of this respect might be the use of Tyrone instead of James when designating the father's speeches throughout the play. The descriptions of the two (the stage parent and the real-life parent) are again almost identical.

The manner of Mary and Tyrone's entrance and their conversation helps the audience to understand them and their relationship. The playful hug which he gives Mary as they enter the living room is both affectionate and protective. The love and affection they feel for one another is indicated throughout the play, and, in the things he says and does, Tyrone seems to be trying to protect Mary. Their "small talk" about her getting too fat and about his digestion at first belies the tension they both feel - and the specter which hovers over the Tyrone household.

Mary's paleness is the first discordant element introduced into the play and of itself is of little importance. But Tyrone's first speech complimenting Mary on the twenty pounds she gained indicates she has been ill. The comment about her lack of appetite at breakfast indicates the husband's continued concern. Somehow the conversation is too gay and trivial, too casual and unimportant. At this point in the play there is only the very slightest undercurrent of concern, unrest, and anxiety - but this will grow in intensity as the play and the day progress.

From the dining room the voices of Jamie and Edmund are heard. Mary comments that the hired girl, Cathleen, must be waiting to clear the table; Tyrone comments that they are probably hatching some scheme to get money from him. They discuss his speculations in real estate but, hearing a fit of coughing, the conversation turns to Edmund's "summer cold."

Comment

Here we see Tyrone's concern with money - the boys' scheme "to touch the Old Man"; the cheap cigar he's enjoying; the real estate bargains that don't quite come off. But more important than the concern with money or the concern with Edmund's health, is the father's concern that the mother not be upset. And when he expresses his concern, Mary is quick to deny her anxiety. Neither wants to admit it, but there is something bothering both of them which they dare not or cannot discuss.

Mary says his continued concern about her health is making her self-conscious; he replies that he is just so glad to have her back, "her old dear self again." Gazing out of the window she remarks the fog is gone - she couldn't get much sleep with the foghorn going all night. Hearing the boys laughing, she calls them into the living room.

Comment

O'Neill is slowly revealing more and more about the Tyrones, especially Mary, and yet there is an aura of mystery about just what is wrong. Tyrone tells her that she has to take care of herself, that she seems a bit high-strung, that it's wonderful to have her back, "her old dear self again." And because the audience can sense that something is wrong, Mary's protests that she's fine do not ring true.

21

The first reference to the fog is made during this brief exchange. The presence of fog helps us to "picture" the setting of the house, but it also provides a physical manifestation of the haze or cloud hanging over the Tyrone family. Like the seemingly casual, unimportant remarks at the very beginning of this scene, the fog and the references to the fog grow in significance and importance as the play develops.

Before Jamie and Edmund actually appear, enough is said about them to indicate the animosity between them and the father, the condition of Edmund's health, and the mother's favoring of Jamie. When Mary wonders aloud what they are laughing about, Tyrone says it's probably some joke on him. Both of them express concern about Edmund's health. And when the father remarks that Jamie is always sneering at somebody, Mary tells him not to start in on "poor Jamie." (Poor Jamie is nearly thirty-four - Edmund is twenty-four.)

O'Neill's description of the two brothers is interesting not only because they physically resemble Eugene O'Neill (Edmund) and Jamie O'Neill, but also because the descriptions reveal so much about Eugene O'Neill's attitude and feelings about himself and his brother. Jamie is good looking despite "marks of dissipation." His countenance has a "Mephistophelian cast" but he still has the Irish charm of the ne'er-do-well who is attractive to women and popular with men. Edmund looks more like his mother, has her sensitive mouth and hands with exceptionally long fingers; and like his mother, he has the same quality of "extreme nervous sensibility." From his appearance it is apparent he is in poor health.

With the entrance of Jamie and Edmund, the atmosphere becomes more tense, the laughter more forced, and the pleasant atmosphere more difficult to maintain. Edmund relates a humorous experience involving one of Tyrone's tenants, and then leaves to get a book.

From the very beginning, the conversation of the family is forced - the mother's attempt to be gay; Jamie's and Edmund's comments about how well the mother looks; the father's slighting remarks about Jamie. Note also the stage directions - the mother's "merry tone is a bit forced"; Jamie eyes her with "an uneasy, probing look"; Tyrone's remarks are often made "contemptuously" or "scathingly"; Edmund responds "irritably" and attempts to ignore what is said. The tension is mounting - not only is there a certain animosity amongst various ones of the family (primarily between the father and the two sons) but also we "sense" there is a dark secret they all share.

The kidding comments made about Tyrone's snoring almost develop into a full-scale argument - in a humorous vein Jamie quotes Shakespeare, which occasions a scathing remark from the father about the son's interest in the horses; the mother tries to smooth things over; and Edmund shows his irritation of the father's constant picking. Earlier Tyrone remarked that the joke is always "on the Old Man." Here we see the way the family often divides: Jamie and Edmund versus the father, with the mother acting as a peacemaker. Even the account of the humorous incident involving Shaughnessy provokes more disagreement and more futile attempts to maintain the "peace."

As the play develops we will see that each one of them is at least partially justified in the way he feels and reacts in a given situation and to a particular remark. A good part of the ambivalence which the audience feels stems from the partial justification which each has for the way he thinks and acts. O'Neill often wrote his plays in such a way that the audience acts as a jury sitting in judgment - events and ideas are presented and the audience must decide who is right and who is wrong, who is responsible and who isn't.

Mary remarks that his summer cold is making Edmund irritable, but Jamie blurts out that the "Kid is damned sick." Tyrone attempts to pacify Mary's irritation and mentions Dr. Hardy - she scoffs at his name. Aware that they are watching her, Mary fusses with her hair. Tyrone gives her another hug and again compliments her on her good looks - then she goes out to talk to the cook.

Comment

They are all concerned about Edmund's "summer cold" - Jamie thinks his brother is really sick; Mary resents any inference that it might be more than a cold; Tyrone wants to assume that Dr. Hardy's diagnosis (a touch of malarial fever that Edmund had caught when he was in the tropics) is correct. The stage directions indicate that any conversation about illness is verboten - another indication that they are all trying to hide something. Mary's fussing with her hair repeats her previous action when she felt they were looking at her - it is her attempt to "explain" their staring.

Tyrone's affectionate regard for Mary keeps us aware of the deep feeling they have for each other. When he kisses her, the stage directions indicate that one sees in her face "the girl she had once been." Mary's remark that her hair had not begun to turns white until after Edmund was born also recalls the past. This concerns with the past - with the "had been" and "could have been" - receives more and more emphasis as the play develops. (Note that throughout this section Tyrone and Jamie have tried to keep the conversation light and gay.)

As soon as the mother leaves, Jamie and Tyrone begin to argue about the seriousness of Edmund's illness, the miserliness of the Old Man, Jamie's continued failure in life, and the bad influence which the older brother has on Edmund. The one thing they agree on is their mutual concern for the mother.

Comment

The change in the tone, manner, and the tenor of the conversation as soon as the mother leaves indicates that they have tried to maintain some semblance of amiability for her sake. Now Jamie and Tyrone say what they really think - about Edmund, about Mary, and about each other. The discussion centers on Edmund since they both know he probably has consumption (tuberculosis - an often fatal disease in the first part of the 1900s).

When Jamie says Edmund would probably be all right if the father had sent him to a real doctor when he was first taken ill instead of a cheap quack, we recall the earlier references to Tyrone's stinginess. His reply that the only thing Jamie cares about is "whores and whiskey" helps explain the "marks of dissipation" referred to earlier. Tyrone defends his actions by saying that Jamie initiated Edmund into a life of dissipation and this illness is the result. These comments, together with Jamie's recounting of Edmund's experiences as a sailor and bum, are all part of the autobiographical elements in the play.

Jamie's main interest in life is wine, women, and song - and the remarks about Edmund's "following in his footsteps" are all interesting and true. But the most important and most revealing thing about the conversation is the ambivalent feelings Jamie has about Edmund. He says they have been very close (and even the father realizes this) but at the same time Jamie seems to be jealous of his younger brother. The implication here is that perhaps Jamie led Edmund "astray" to prevent his being successful. And since the play is autobiographical, we might infer that O'Neill had such suspicions about his own brother. Jamie's comment that Edmund "does what he wants to do, and to hell with anyone else" would seem to be O'Neill's description of his own attitude.

When Tyrone says Mary needs peace and freedom from worry and that she's been so well in the two months since "she came home," we again wonder what her "illness" is. Our curiosity is aroused even more when Jamie mentions that the night before she had slept in the spare room and that when she starts sleeping alone in there, "it has always been a sign." Since her "illness" is as much mental as physical, when Jamie says that the doctor was to blame, we begin to suspect that the mother is a dope addict.

Not until Act Three does O'Neill actually use the words "dope fiend" and thereby confirm any suspicions we might have had. By keeping us "in suspense" he not only maintains our interest, but he also has the revealing of the plot to the audience duplicate the revealing of the truth to Tyrone, Edmund, and Jamie. At about the same time we are told of her drug addiction, they become certain that she has begun to use drugs again.

Even though they are suspicious, Tyrone, Jamie, and Edmund hope against hope that their suspicions are unfounded - but almost from the beginning they have suspected the truth. Jamie is the first to be suspicious - and when he mentions his suspicions to his father, Tyrone is resentful. Edmund is the last to suspect and the last to know. Ironically they all feel that if they won't admit what they know to be true, it won't be.

Note also the **allusion** that the father makes to Edmund when discussing the possibility of the mother again being addicted. He starts to say that it would be like a curse if worry over Edmund caused her to use drugs again. (It was during her long illness after his birth that she was first given drugs.) Earlier Mary mentioned that her hair started to turn white after Edmund was born. These autobiographical references by O'Neill would seem to indicate that he was beset by guilt-feelings because of his mother's addiction.

Hearing Mary coming, Tyrone and Jamie quickly change the conversation. They tell her they are going to cut the hedge, and they go out, leaving her alone. A few minutes later Edmund comes in. During their conversation the mother mentions some of her concerns: Edmund's health, the house which she doesn't like, her loneliness, Tyrone's miserliness. In attempting to answer her, Edmund makes reference to her "illness"; knowing that they suspect the truth (that she is again using drugs) she becomes even more bitter and resentful than before.

Comment

The sudden change in conversation and tone of voice is noted by Mary - she is suspicious of the others as they are of her. She tells them if they are going to work on the hedge they should take advantage of the sunshine before the fog comes back - and adds, "Because I know it will." Because a number of references are made to the fog, we had best discuss its significance for the play and for O'Neill.

Fog is a hazy condition in the atmosphere which impairs visibility and obscures reality. In this play O'Neill uses the fog as a symbol for the whole Tyrone family, but most especially the mother. When the play opens, the fog is just clearing and the outlook is bright; before the play ends, the fog will return with the resulting gloom. These atmospheric conditions correspond to the family's change of attitude, from one of hope to one of despair. (It is interesting to note that one of the first plays O'Neill wrote was entitled "Fog.")

Just before he goes out, Jamie tells his mother they're all proud of her and happy, but that she has to be careful. Mary replies with a stubborn, bitterly resentful look and says she doesn't know what he means. Although both know the truth, they are afraid to admit it to themselves or to each other. Mary is desperate now and her only defense is to show her defiance and resentment of any **allusion** to what she knows to be true.

When Edmund comes in, his remarks echo Jamie's: "You take care of yourself. That's all that counts." And when he tells her she must be on her guard because of "what happened before," Mary again shows her bitterness and resentment. But more important than this are Mary's remarks which indicate her dissatisfaction with her life, her home, and her family. And her dissatisfaction with her present life makes her yearn all the more for her former, happy life at the convent.

Mary says that they are all spying on her, that they don't trust her, that it would serve them right if their suspicions were true. Edmund tries to pacify her and allays her fears; Mary replies that she's not blaming him - that is what makes it so hard "for all of us. We can't forget." Edmund goes to join the others, leaving Mary alone. As the scene ends, she sits, her long fingers drumming on the arms of the chair, "driven by an insistent life of their own, without her consent."

Comment

Two important points are stressed again in this section - the mutual suspicion, and the inability to forget. From their conversation we realize that Edmund too suspects that his mother has lapsed again into drug addiction.

Mary's comment that "we can't forget" refers not only to their remembering her former, unsuccessful attempts to break the drug habit but also to her remembrance of things past - especially her life in the convent school. (The references to the convent mean the boarding school she attended.) The **irony** in this and other **episodes** results from the attempts of the characters to act normal in an abnormal situation and to say one thing when they mean another.

O'Neill's final comment at the end of this act when he speaks of her drumming fingers "driven by an insistent life of their own, without her consent" introduces his concern with the Forces that shape men's souls and men's lives. Although he could not explain it nor define it, he often referred to it in his plays and in his commentary on his own work. In a letter to Arthur Hobson Quinn written in 1925 he said, "I'm always acutely conscious of the force behind - (Fate, God, our biological past creating our present, whatever one calls it - Mystery certainly) - and of the eternal tragedy of Man in his glorious, self-destructive struggle to make the Force express him instead of being, as an animal is, an infinitesimal incident in its expression." (See *A History of the American Drama from the Civil War to the Present Day,* Volume II, New York, 1945, p. 199.) More about this Force later.

LONG DAY'S JOURNEY INTO NIGHT

ACT II - IV

. . . .

ACT II - SCENE 1

As the scene opens, it is just after noon of the same day; Edmund is sitting alone in the living room when Cathleen, the hired girl, enters carrying a tray laden with bourbon, whiskey glasses, and ice water. They make small-talk - and she leaves to call the others to lunch.

Comment

O'Neill's comment when setting the scene notes a change which has taken place since the play opened - no sunlight comes into the room now and there is a faint haziness in the air. As commented on earlier, the fog or haze which obscures reality parallels the attempts of each member of the family to obscure or hide reality. As Edmund sits reading, he listens for some sound from upstairs, knowing but at the same time attempting to deny the truth about his mother.

Cathleen's flippant and quite humorous remarks in this encounter with Edmund relieve the tension which has been building up since the beginning of the play. There is an **irony** in her remarks since they "mean more" to the audience than they do to her. She says that neither Edmund nor Mister Jamie will ever be as good looking as the father (another symbol of conflict between the father and the sons); that Mister Jamie wouldn't miss the time to stop work if he had a watch to his name (he's completely dependent on the father); and that the mother is lying down in the spare room (where she usually goes when taking drugs).

While Edmund is sneaking a drink, Jamie comes in, and he has one with him. (They fill the bottle with water so the father won't know.) They discuss Edmund's illness and the mother's actions and comments that morning. Hearing her coming they grow tense with a hopeful, fearful expectancy.

Comment

This **episode** with the whiskey bottle expresses the camaraderie of the two brothers and again shows them united to outwit the father. Note also the secretiveness of Edmund's attempt to take a drink and the care with which they replace the liquid in the bottle. Much of the activity carried on by the Tyrone family is under-handed and sneaky - in great things and in small. They are forever attempting to put something over on somebody - and thus obscure the truth.

When they discuss the mother, Edmund resents Jamie's hinting that she might have gone back to her old habit; and Jamie reprimands Edmund for not staying with her all morning. Although they both think (or know) that she has started using dope again, they don't want to have to admit it. Because Tyrone, Jamie, and Edmund all try so hard to deny the truth and to blame each other or the mother for her affliction, it appears that they all feel some guilt and some responsibility for what has happened to her -and to themselves.

O'Neill was much concerned with life-illusion, or the attempt of an individual to mold himself and his reality according to his own designs. It is not simply a question of the individual lying to himself -instead it is the individual making his reality conform to his desires. O'Neill expressed it thus: "One's outer life passes in a solitude haunted by the masks of others; one's inner life passes in a solitude haunted by the masks of oneself." (See "Memoranda in Masks," *American Spectator Year-book,* (New York, 1934), p. 161.)

Mary enters the living room - she seems less nervous but she seems detached in her voice and manner and somewhat withdrawn. Jamie and Edmund suspect the worst although they make some attempt to act and speak as if everything is all right. Jamie makes a sneering remark about the father, and Mary reprimands him for it. She says, "None of us can help the things life has done to us."

Comment

Mary's actions and attitude indicate that she is withdrawing more and more into herself and under the influence of narcotics. She hopes they will not notice, but Edmund is immediately suspicious and Jamie's cynical, embittered expression reveals his comprehension of what has happened. But "they act out their parts" as they have done before and will undoubtedly have to do again.

When Mary rebukes Jamie for his sneering remark concerning the father, her comment about what "life has done to us" again brings in the idea of Forces alluded to earlier. If you believe that you are predestined or directed by some Force over which you have no control, free-will and self-responsibility are eliminated. When one is not responsible, one is not to blame - and thus Mary (and O'Neill) are able to justify themselves and their actions.

Cathleen tells them that lunch is ready and goes out to call Tyrone. Jamie insinuates that the mother has broken her promise again - and Edmund curses him for even thinking such a thing. Tyrone comes in while Mary is in the kitchen, and Jamie hints at what has happened.

Comment

When Jamie accuses the mother, she says you can't help being what the past has made you. Even when confronted with the truth (that the mother is using drugs), they all still try to act as if everything were all right - to deny the reality and live in illusion.

When Mary returns, she prattles on about the lunch, and the house, and their life together, and the past. Because they look at her accusingly, she fusses with her hair self-consciously. Finally, when the parents are alone, Tyrone remarks that he had been a fool ever to have believed she could stop using drugs.

Comment

Mary's comments reveal not only her drifting away from reality but also her continued concern with the past. She says she's sick of pretending that theirs is a home - that they never should have married - that then nothing would ever have happened. But in spite of everything she tries to keep up the pretense of normalcy and, in spite of Tyrone's accusations, says she doesn't know what he is talking about.

The positions of the characters at the close of this scene parallel their positions at the beginning of the play - the two boys in the dining room and Tyrone and Mary in the living room. But there the similarity of the two scenes ends, for the opening scene was one of hope but this scene is one of despair. Notice also the change in the attitude and demeanor of Tyrone. The vigorous, self-satisfied, happy husband has become a dejected, angry old man.

ACT II - SCENE 2

With lunch finished, they come back into the living room - first Mary, then Tyrone and the boys. She chats on about inconsequential things which none of them care about - all thought is concentrated on her "condition." When Dr. Hardy telephones, Mary remarks that it was a cheap quack like him that first gave her the "Medicine."

Comment

Again O'Neill's stage directions reveal much about the characters, their thoughts, and their attitudes before a single word is spoken. Tyrone, disgusted and weary, avoids his wife as much as possible. Jamie's face shows the cynicism he feels, and Edmund is just heartsick. And Mary - she is in a world of her own. They all act as if they are waiting for something to happen - and in a sense they are.

Mary rambles on about the cook, and their house that isn't a home, and the lonely hotel rooms, and the "what-used-to-be." Again O'Neill shows concern with the past and with Mary's desire to "go back." There is an interesting parallel in Mary's attempt to "go back" by taking drugs to forget the present and O'Neill's attempt to "go back" by recreating these scenes of his youth.

After Mary leaves to go upstairs, Jamie remarks, "Another shot in the arm!" Tyrone and Edmund reprimand him, but all agree that she has started again. Disgusted with the constant bickering and fighting, Edmund goes out.

Comment

Because Mary knows they don't trust her, she taunts them before she goes upstairs, and tells them they're welcome to come up and watch if they're suspicious. Tyrone replies that he's not a jailer and this isn't a "prison." Ironically in a sense it is a prison for all of them because they are caught in a web of circumstance and are under the influence of Forces-Fate, God, biological past - which control and shape their destinies. Along these same lines, Croswell Bowen commented thus: "In the end the characters stand self-revealed, and the audience knows and feels that this family is bound together by ties of love and hate and need." (See *The Curse of the Misbegotten*, McGraw-Hill, 1959, pp. 272-273.)

When the three attempt to fathom why the mother has fallen back into the habit again, their comments reflect the thinking and philosophy of each. Jamie says there is no cure and that they were saps to hope; Edmund indicates that it's fate and that there is nothing they can do about it; Tyrone believes that if Mary again had faith (belief in the doctrines of the Catholic Church) she would have the spirit needed to fight against the "curse." Note that Tyrone equates the philosophy Jamie got from "broadway loafers" and the one Edmund got from his books - he thinks both are "rotten to the core."

Tyrone tells Jamie that Edmund has consumption and has to go to a sanitarium. Jamie tells him to send Edmund to a good place and not some "cheap dump."

Comment

Again the references to Tyrone's stinginess, and notice that the father says he can't "throw money away." There is also a sardonic humor in the father's remark that everyone on his side of the family had lungs as "strong as an ox"; he appears to take Edmund's illness as a personal affront.

As Jamie leaves, Mary comes in and remarks on the weather- it's getting hazier out so they're in for another night of fog. The father tries to excuse himself to go to the Club - Mary comments that she'll be alone again. Bitter at her relapse, Tyrone remarks that he spent a lot of money he couldn't afford to help her. Mary tries to pacify him and says they "must not try to understand what we cannot understand, or help things that cannot be helped - the things life has done to us we cannot excuse or explain." Then she mentions again that she was healthy before Edmund was born.

Comment

Again the reference to fog here has the double meaning - referring both to the atmosphere and to the family. Now that they both know she is taking dope again, their remarks are more caustic and their rebuttals more cutting. Mary says he'll come home drunk, and he says no man had better reason. She says they will all go out and leave her soon, and he says she is "leaving" them. She mentions his former mistress, and he mentions the night she ran out of the house half-crazy. And so it goes - each trying to hurt the other because each has been hurt. The comment that the things "life has done to us we cannot excuse or explain" again indicates that Mary feels no responsibility for what has happened - it is fate or Forces that no one can understand.

When Mary recounts events from the past, we see how all the Tyrones share the blame for the way the family is (or at least in her mind they do). Jamie is blamed for Eugene's death; Edmund's birth caused her sickness; the father's miserliness prompted him to get a cheap doctor who prescribed dope. Recalling that Jamie in a sense "started the whole thing," Mary remarks, "I've never been able to forgive him for that." Although she very often defends Jamie before his father, her action might well be an attempt to compensate for the animosity she still feels towards him. Throughout the play these ambiguous feelings of the characters and the conflicts inherent therein are stressed.

Mary's comments about Edmund (which are actually O'Neill's comments about himself) are interesting and revealing. She says, "He has never been happy. He never will be." A number of critics would say that O'Neill's personal unhappiness prompted him to write "morbid" and "depressing" plays.

Edmund comes into the living room before going to see the doctor and, much to his surprise, Tyrone gives him ten dollars. After the father leaves, Edmund appeals to the mother to stop while she still has a chance - but she is already too far gone. As the scene closes, she is sitting alone.

Comment

O'Neill rarely misses an opportunity to show in the conversation and action of the Tyrone family the conflict which each feels internally regarding the others. Tyrone gives Edmund ten dollars - but must add a sarcastic comment. Edmund is genuinely pleased and grateful but then adds cynically, "Did Doc Hardy tell you I was going to die?" When Edmund tells Mary that they will all help her if she'll only try, she replies that the doctor told her before she came home that she must not be upset and all she's done is worry about him. Somehow none of them can do or say anything without hurting the others - usually on purpose.

Mary again recollects her days at the convent and her faith in the Blessed Virgin - she yearns for the peace and security she once knew. Mary's very last speech as she sits alone again illustrates the conflict and uncertainty which each feels - first she says she's lonely; then she admits she's lying and that she's glad they're gone.

ACT III

It is about six-thirty, the fog is rolling in from the Sound, and Mary and Cathleen are in the living room. Mary talks about herself, her early life, the family - Cathleen prattles on about the chauffeur and the cook and her own concerns; only rarely does either know or understand what the other has said.

Comment

As the scene opens, the spectacle of Cathleen holding a whiskey glass, which she has apparently emptied, and Mary, chattering like a happy school girl, is at the same time humorous and pathetic. Both are somewhat out of contact with reality - Cathleen because of whiskey and Mary because of narcotics. Their conversation provides more background material on the family and again emphasizes the importance of the past; but neither really understands nor cares what the other says or thinks.

In this scene Mary says she loves the fog because "it hides you from the world and the world from you," but she hates the foghorns because they warn you and call you back. (Perhaps for Mary the fog is like the narcotics which obscure reality and the foghorns are the family's warnings.) We are told that the "rheumatism medicine" (narcotics) stops "all the pain." This emphasis on all reiterates Mary's dissatisfaction with her present life and her longing for her past life. She tells Cathleen that the medicine kills the pain and that only "the past when you were happy is real."

Note that neither one is really communicating with the other -Mary isn't listening to what Cathleen says and Cathleen doesn't understand what Mary is saying. This lack of communication parallels the lack of communication among the various members of the family. Another parallel is in Cathleen's whiskey-drinking; the Tyrone men drink to help forget the realities of life. All of them are trying to "escape" from something, each other, or themselves.

Cathleen leaves to help with dinner and Mary sits alone - an old, cynical, embittered woman - and tries to pray. Hearing Edmund and Tyrone coming, she becomes at the same time resentful and relieved. The father and son realize at once that the mother has drifted still further away from reality.

Comment

With Mary under the influence of narcotics and Edmund and Tyrone under the influence of alcohol, no one is guarded in comment or kind in attitude - each says what he thinks with little regard for the feelings of the others. Before there was some attempt to maintain a semblance of decorum and decency, but now the facade is torn away. Mary says that Jamie wants to make Edmund a failure like himself; when the mother says Edmund would cry "at the drop of a hat," he says he must have guessed there was a good reason not to laugh; and when Tyrone attempts to defend himself against her accusations, he says that when she has the poison in her, she wants to blame everyone but herself.

But in spite of everything, the love which Tyrone and Mary feel for each other remains strong. And that is a great part of the **irony** in the play - in spite of their love for each other, or perhaps because of it, they continually hurt each other.

When Tyrone leaves to get another bottle of whiskey, Edmund tells his mother he has to go to a sanitarium. She refuses to listen to him. Heartbroken he rushes from the room.

Comment

When Mary tries to explain why Tyrone acts and believes as he does, Edmund says he's heard it all before. The mother's reply expresses the common family failing: "Yes, dear, you've had to listen but I don't think you've ever tried to understand." This lack of understanding, the inability or unwillingness to communicate, is at the root of much of the family's unhappiness and distrust. Although O'Neill here presents this lack of understanding as a failing of the Tyrone family, it is a failing common to the majority of mankind.

In this conversation Edmund tells when he learned for sure of his mother's addiction and comments, "God, it made everything in life seem rotten." He admits that he knew, but that he tried to make believe it wasn't true - he preferred illusion to reality; he preferred uncertainty to certainty. Edmund's comment that "it made everything in life seem rotten" could of course be considered O'Neill's comment regarding his own mother's addiction. And when Edmund makes cutting remarks to Mary it is O'Neill cutting remarks to his mother.

Tyrone returns and Mary says she thinks Edmund is going to die, that it would have been better if Edmund had never been born, that then he wouldn't hate her for being a dope fiend. Just before Cathleen comes in to call them to dinner, Tyrone tells her that Edmund understands that it was a curse put on her. She goes upstairs, and he goes in to dinner alone.

Comment

When discussing the characters in this play, Frederic I. Carpenter wrote: "Although each major character is realized in action and in speech, his inner nature is never finally determined." (See *Eugene O'Neill*, Twayne Publisher, Inc., 1964, p. 152.) This statement is certainly justified by the ambiguity which is presented again and again in the characters' speech and action. In this scene, after Tyrone wrathfully declares that Jamie tried to pick the lock to get at the whiskey, the father smugly adds that "he fooled him though." The inference is that the father enjoys a kind of "battle of wits" with the sons. The audience must begin to wonder if the characters actually enjoy the pain and the misery they cause one another and endure themselves.

ACT IV

As the scene opens it is about midnight - Tyrone sits playing solitaire, the fog horn and ship's bells sounding in the distance. Edmund enters, having tripped in the dark hall, and they argue about the father's cheapness.

Comment

O'Neill's concern in setting the scene draws the viewer's attention to a number of the things he wishes to emphasize. The stage is dark with only the reading lamp on the table lighted. The dimness of the scene parallels the all-enveloping gloom, as does the fog which is "denser than ever." The foghorn recalls the mother's comment about its being a warning, or signal of danger; the ships' bells introduce the possibility of release or escape - a means to get away (which O'Neill had once used himself). The two bottles of whiskey indicate the father's attempt to escape by forgetting, but the stage directions indicate that he is still "possessed by hopeless resignation." And in this act where much is revealed, Tyrone wears a pince-nez, an aid to better vision, recalling Mary's inability to find her glasses.

In this scene a considerable amount of the action and dialogue concerns the lights - the hall lamp, the reading lamp, and the bulbs in the chandelier. Because the father's stinginess has been stressed throughout, Tyrone's desire to turn out the lights is understandable and "in character"; the stage business concerned with turning the bulbs in the chandelier on and off provokes laughter and relieves the tension. But more important than either is the use of lights to symbolize the knowledge and understanding Edmund is gaining about the others and himself. (Remember, for all the Tyrones this has been a long day's journey into night, but for Edmund it becomes in the last analysis, a long day's journey into light.)

When Edmund leaves the hall light on, it provokes the father's angers and provides the impetus for a heated exchange which increases our knowledge and understanding of both father and son. Tyrone will not listen to Edmund's reasonable comments about the cost of electricity - he believes only what he wants to believe. When Edmund doesn't obey, the father threatens to thrash him. The father is pictured as an unreasonable tyrant who demands unquestioning obedience. Remembering Edmund's illness, the father relents and then proceeds to turn on the three bulbs in the chandelier overhead, commenting that they'll probably "all end up in the poorhouse."

Edmund tells the father he walked out to the beach to be alone with himself. He recites poetry which expresses his beliefs and feelings - Tyrone comments that Shakespeare said everything worth saying.

Comment

During this part of Act IV, the overhead lights illuminate the characters physically even as the dialogue illuminates them psychologically. And, like the light from the bare bulbs, the dialogue is glaring and unshielded. Note that near the end of their dialogue, Tyrone turns out the lights because they hurt his eyes; but, when Jamie comes in, the older brother turns the bulbs on again and proceeds to reveal himself literally and figuratively.

When told that he should have more sense than to walk out in the fog, Edmund replies with a quotation from Ernest Dowson (English poet, 1867-1900), part of which reads as follows:

> They are not long, the days of wine and roses: Out of a misty dream Our path emerges for a while, then closes within a dream.

Since this is the first of a number of quotations, it, in a sense, sets the tone for the whole act.

The first line indicates the brevity of life - the three remaining lines indicate the mystical and mysterious elements of life. The concern with "misty dreams" repeats the fog **imagery** alluded to earlier. And if we emerge from a dream and then our life closes within a dream, there is no meaning to life and no purpose to existence. We cannot understand or explain whence we come or whither we are going.

Edmund proceeds to comment further on life saying he wants to be where "truth is untrue and life can hide from itself." This desire to shun the truth and to hide from reality repeats the attempts of all of them to live in illusion by forgetting what is and was. When Edmund speaks of escaping reality by walking on the "bottom of the sea," he is repeating exactly the words of Henrik Ibsen (Norwegian dramatist, 1828-1906) in his play concerning the necessity of having a "life-illusion," *The Wild Duck*.

Edmund, the sensitive, perceptive youth who has a touch of the poet in him, at the same time impresses and depresses the father with his morbid ruminations. Tyrone cites Shakespeare as having the most worthwhile ideas, "We are such stuff as dreams are made on, and our little life is rounded with a sleep." (Shakespeare's *The Tempest*, Act IV, Scene I) But Edmund sardonically substitutes manure for dreams. This substitution brings us very much "down-to-earth." The attempt to substitute illusion for reality, to escape into another world, is short-lived. For a few moments one may be blissfully unaware of himself and those around him, but very soon he may decide that his life and his dreams are "manure." O'Neill's choice of word here is "morbidly poetic" since he likens life to an animal's excrement. With his next quotation, Edmund again return to his concern with illusion.

Since both father and son are trying to "drown their troubles" in drink, Edmund quotes a translation of a Baudelaire (French poet, 1821-1867) prose poem: "Be always drunken. . . . With wine, with poetry, or with virtue, as you will." To escape the horrible burden of time, the poet says to be always drunken-to be so sated that one is not conscious of the horror of reality. One may escape by wine-drugging the mind (by whiskey or narcotics, for instance); by poetry-losing oneself in beauty; by virtue - finding release in an ideal.

They talk of Jamie, and Edmund recites from Baudelaire's "Epilogue." Tyrone tells Edmund his taste in literature is for "filth and despair and pessimism"; he calls the authors in Edmund's library "whoremongers and degenerates."

Comment

When Edmund quotes Baudelaire's poem he says it is about Jamie and Broadway. The concluding lines are:

> I love thee, infamous city! Harlots and hunted have pleasures of their own to give, The vulgar herd can never understand.

Significantly the poem recognizes and praises evil - biographers have noted that O'Neill long admired his older brother, and even after he recognized the harm that he had done, the younger brother was still morbidly fascinated by him. The extent of Jamie's influence will be seen later in this act.

After Tyrone comments that the son's taste in literature is for "filth and despair and pessimism," Edmund says that when Jamie is drunk he often recites poetry to some fat whore who doesn't understand what he is saying. There is a parallel between the fat whore who suspects she's being insulted because she doesn't understand what Jamie is saying and the father who believes that if you deny God, you deny hope. Both are face-to-face with ideas, concepts, and concerns that the "vulgar herd can never understand," and for each the line of defense is to "take offense." When Tyrone recites the names of the authors in Edmund's library, we are given a list of writers whom O'Neill sometimes imitated, often read, and always admired. A brief comment about each will help to indicate why Tyrone called them madmen, fools, and atheists, and why Edmund (O'Neill) felt a kinship with them:

Voltaire (French satirist, 1694-1778) was a champion of progress and liberty and a firm believer in freedom of speech.

Rousseau (French writer, 1712-1778) believed that the "natural man" is happy and good but that "civilization" corrupts him; he stressed the importance of the individual.

Schopenhauer (German philosopher, 1778-1860) believed suffering was necessary to make existence worthwhile and that the ultimate reality is the will.

Ibsen (Norwegian dramatist, 1828-1906) wrote realistic dramas which employed much symbolism in depicting the individual's inner conflicts.

Baudelaire (French poet, 1821-1867) in his poetry attempted to extract beauty from ugliness and to portray the paradox of the existence of good and evil in man.

Whitman (American poet, 1819-1892) celebrated Man in all his aspects and condemned nothing; he boasted of being the poet of the body and the soul.

Poe (American writer, 1809-1849) wrote with great perception of abnormal states of mind and the subconscious self.

Zola (French novelist, 1840-1902) attempted to create "real" characters whose actions were in accordance with psychology, sociology, heredity, and environment.

Hearing the mother moving around upstairs, Tyrone tells Edmund he shouldn't pay too much attention to her tales of the past. The father says, "Remember she's not responsible," and Edmund replies that it was the father's stinginess that's responsible. Charge and countercharge are hurled back and forth.

Comment

When Tyrone tells Edmund to take the mother's comments about the past with a grain of salt, we see an example of how two people can look at the same thing but "see" the thing very differently. The mother considered her former home "wonderful," her father "noble," her convent days the "happiest," her piano playing "outstanding," her desire to be a nun "sincere." But the father says that she was mistaken, that she didn't see things as they really were. O'Neill probably felt that these memories were the illusion the mother needed to make reality tolerable; as she remarked earlier, her medicine kills the pain so she can go back to the past when she was really happy. (Remember Edmund - O'Neill's alter ego - is described as being like his mother.) Edmund remarks that the mother builds a wall around herself, a bank of fog in which she hides; a little earlier he remarked that he loved the fog.

One of the primary sources of the conflict in this play is the ambiguous feelings which each has for the other members of the family. John Henry Raleigh commented, "Love for all of the Tyrones is ambiguous, unresolved tension between tenderness and hate, sentimentality and irony." (See "O'Neill's *Long Day's Journey into Night* and New England Irish-Catholicism," *Partisan Review* XXVI, No. 4. (Fall 1957) 584.) Edmund, speaking of his mother, says it's as if "in spite of loving us, she hated us!" Certainly a great part of this ambiguity arises from the way in which each views himself, the others, and the actions of all. Throughout the play the abrupt changes in the tone and tenor of the conversation express this ambiguity.

At this point in the play when Edmund reiterates the father's culpability for the mother's condition because of his stinginess, we must consider the validity of his assumptions. Since the play is autobiographical, is this a true picture of O'Neill's father? Why is reference again and again made to the father's stinginess? Should the father's stinginess be considered symbolic?

Biographers tend to agree that James O'Neill, Sr., was inclined to be conservative and thrifty in many ways. His impoverished background and the vivid memories of his mother struggling to support a family contributed to the high esteem in which he held money. But there is really no proof that he ever hesitated to provide whatever was needed for or by his family. The cheap hotel rooms and bad food which the mother referred to earlier would be often the lot of any travelling troupe (which the *Monte Cristo* company was). Records indicate that the family's summer home was built at considerable expense. And when Eugene was taken ill, the father did call in a specialist. We might safely assume that the stinginess of the father was exaggerated in this play; we might also safely assume that the stinginess of the father was symbolic.

To be stingy means to be covetous or to be unwilling to give, and certainly all the Tyrones were covetous and unwilling to give of themselves. They were stingy with their affections and in their regard for one another; each was self-seeking, and this characteristic was often detrimental to the well-being of the others. The label "stingy" is applied to the father but it is also applicable to all the Tyrones. By using "stinginess" as a leitmotif, the play is given unity and an important concept and concern is emphasized.

During this part of the conversation, Edmund says you have to "make allowances in this damned family or go nuts!" Once he realizes that life involves "give and take," that one must "live and let live," that "to err is human, and to forgive divine," Edmund moves a little closer to the light. (As noted earlier, he is the only one enlightened by this day's experiences.) Notice he says damned family, not damn family - again emphasizing the influence of some outside Force over which they have no control.

They talk of the son's adventures and the father's early life; Tyrone tells Edmund that the play that brought him such great financial success ruined him. Edmund admits that he is happy and free only when he forgets his fears and hopes and dreams and belongs to Life itself. Hearing Jamie coming, Tyrone goes out on the porch.

Comment

This whole act contains many autobiographical references - at this point Tyrone's references to Edmund's adventures relate directly to O'Neill's own early life. And when the father admits that the play that made him financially, ruined him artistically, the play meant is *Monte Cristo*. Significantly, Edmund (O'Neill) comments that now he knows the father a lot better. Evidently, O'Neill late in life realized that his father also had been tormented by the "might-have-been." (At the beginning of his career, the critics did liken the senior O'Neill to the great actor, Edwin Booth.)

When Edmund talks of his memories, he says they are all connected with the sea. He tells the father of the few times he lost himself and belonged to Life itself, seeing the secret and being a part of the secret, but that after a moment the fog again obscured him and he moved into darkness, going nowhere and for no good reason. This lack of direction and lack of purpose a number of critics contend resulted from O'Neill's loss of faith in God and the Catholic Church - undoubtedly Tyrone would agree with this view.

When the father remarks that the son has the makings of a poet, Edmund replies that the best he can do is stammer. This comment is often quoted as an indication that O'Neill recognized his own shortcomings as a writer. Perhaps this is true. Certainly O'Neill did not hesitate to tell the truth in this play. But more important than his comment is his belief that he is one of the "fog people"; that he is, therefore, in some way set apart and different - that for this reason his native eloquence is stammering.

Jamie comes in, very apparently drunk, and turns on the three bulbs in the chandelier. He recounts his evening with Fat Violet. Then Jamie confesses why he had tried to make a bum out of Edmund.

Comment

When Jamie and Edmund talk about the father, we find the younger son attempting to defend or at least explain Tyrone's actions and ideas. Again Edmund's growing in knowledge and understanding is emphasized. But Jamie remains the same, if not worse, and when he calls his mother a "hophead" Edmund slugs him.

This scene with the two brothers, played under the glare of the overhead lights, reveals much about their relationship and about O'Neill's feelings regarding his own brother. Probably most important (because Jamie says it and O'Neill evidently thought it) is the fact that the elder brother was jealous of the younger. Jamie tried to make a bum out of Edmund so that the younger brother's success would not make his own failure look even worse. This is another example of an attempt to create or maintain the "life-illusion."

During this conversation, O'Neill has Jamie make a statement similar to Edmund's earlier comment. Having explained the reasons for his actions, Jamie says that he loves Edmund more than he hates him. Again the concern with the ambiguous emotions which the Tyrones feel. (Very often during this act O'Neill repeats particular **themes** and comments in order to emphasize again and again their importance.)

When Tyrone comes back in, he and Jamie begin to argue. Suddenly the light goes on in the front parlor, and the three of them hear the mother playing the piano. Presently she comes in, trailing her old wedding gown.

Comment

When Jamie recites from Rossetti (English poet, 1828-1882), we can apply the words to all the Tyrones except Edmund: "My name is Might-Have-Been; I am also called No More, Too Late, Farewell." For them there is no escape from the night; the sounding of the piano is like a death knell for their hopes and dreams.

As the play nears its conclusion, the mother is reintroduced. During this whole act the audience has been aware of her presence upstairs, but she is not seen. But like some mysterious Force, her influence is felt. Now that each of the characters has been revealed and stripped bare, she returns. Before we may have felt that her "condition" was responsible for their attitudes and actions, but now we know that each is responsible for himself and for each other - no one person is to blame.

Mary has completely reverted to the past: she remarks that Sister Theresa will scold her because she hasn't practiced her lessons. She speaks to Tyrone but gives no sign of recognizing him. She is looking for something, but she doesn't know what. She talks to herself about her life in the convent and the fact that she left to marry James Tyrone and was "so happy for a time."

Comment

After Jamie's initial derogatory comment about the mother being mad, the three sit and stare at her dumbfounded. Tyrone takes and holds the wedding gown; Jamie recites briefly from Swinburne's "A Leavetaking"; and Edmund sits and says nothing. There is nothing that anyone can do or say. Symbolically Mary is looking for something, but she doesn't know what it is. She says that she would die if it were lost because then there would be no hope. Once again the concern with life-illusion, with the necessity of continuing even if we don't know where we are going or why.

Part of the Swinburne poem Jamie recites contains these words.

There is no help for all these things are so, And all the world is bitter as a tear.

Since this is O'Neill speaking through Jamie, we again see the concern with fate, with Forces we cannot control. The bitterness of the world and of our life in the world accounts for our attempts to escape through illusion - or as O'Neill quoted earlier, "Be always drunken....With wine, with poetry, or with virtue, as you will."

LONG DAY'S JOURNEY INTO NIGHT

CHARACTER ANALYSES

Because the play is autobiographical it is not enough simply to discuss the characters, what they do and why they do it. Because the characters are based on O'Neill's family and on himself, we must keep in mind what we already know about them. And because O'Neill is writing about his own flesh and blood, we must realize that his vision was not always clear, his judgment not always unbiased, and his ability to recall particulars not always infallible.

But having said all this, we also keep in mind that although the play is based on reality, it is not supposed to be reality. O'Neill speaks of it as a "play of old sorrow, written in tears and blood," and because it is a play it follows certain dramatic **conventions** and techniques. Although the characters are based on O'Neill's family, they are not O'Neill's family. Certain mental, physical, spiritual, and emotional qualities may be recognized in both the Tyrone family and the O'Neill family, but the emphasis given to particular qualities or characteristics may be quite different.

Writing about the play in the November 18, 1956, edition of the *New York Times*, Brooks Atkinson wrote, "It epitomizes in one terrible day in 1912 the tensions, anxieties and obsessions of a doomed family." Certainly the adjective doomed is well-chosen, but we must not think that the O'Neills thought of themselves as doomed. At one point in the play Mary says, "None of us can help the things life has done to us," but there is no reason to think that O'Neill's mother ever expressed a similar view. In the play Mary Tyrone says this because the dramatist wishes to develop his own point of view and to express his own beliefs. If the play and the characters are "true," they are "true" only in so far as O'Neill is able to ascertain and express what is "true."

JAMES TYRONE

The father is sixty-five but looks ten years younger. He is handsome and vigorous, self-made man proud of himself and his achievements. As a matinee idol he has won the affection and esteem of a large theatre-going public - but his private life causes him much anguish and dismay. A simple, unpretentious man of Irish peasant stock he finds himself at a loss to understand or accept his family's weaknesses and grievances. Although a wealthy man, he is pictured as being stingy, and this stinginess is presented as his dominating trait.

O'Neill's choice of a surname for the family emphasizes the autobiographical element - the name O'Neill had been borne by the kings of Ireland and Shane O'Neill was Earl of Tyrone and King of Ireland. (Eugene O'Neill named his second son Shane.) There is also a planned or accidental ironic twist in the appellation of a proud Irish king being borne by his stingy and narrow-minded descendant. (This may or may not have been O'Neill's intention.)

Henry Hewes writing in the November 24, 1956, issue of the *Saturday Review* made this comment about the family: "Each of the quartet advances from morning's surface jocularity into evening's soul-shaking revelations of self-truth. Each tries to blame others for his or her failures." This is certainly the case with Tyrone. Act 1 begins with his jovial and seemingly carefree entrance with Mary - their conversation concerns the little things which husband and wife share. Even the comment about the boys hatching some scheme "to touch the Old Man" contains little rancor. But before long his bitterness and animosity towards Jamie are revealed and the father's self-righteousness is made apparent.

Note how quickly Tyrone takes offense at any remark that is even slightly disparaging. The simplest thing is enough to set him off and produce a torrent of scathing comments - usually directed at Jamie. These references to what the eldest son has done or has failed to do provide the necessary background material for the audience and also at least partially justify the father's attitude. Because the father is at least partially justified, the problem of who is to blame for what is even more difficult to ascertain. (This is one reason why O'Neill would have difficulty "telling the truth.")

Tyrone changes very little during the play - he understands no more at the end than he does at the beginning. Regardless of what has happened to the others or to himself, he continues to believe that what he thinks is right. During the last act he tells Edmund that the play which made him financially ruined him artistically, but this revelation is more a statement of fact than an admission of mistaken judgment. To the end Tyrone retains faith in himself and the rightness of his judgment. He has no qualms of conscience about what has happened - unable

to protest or unable to understand, he quietly accepts what has
come to pass.

MARY CAVAN TYRONE

The mother is fifty-four, attractive, with large dark eyes and
white hair. But her femininity belies the influence she wields
over the family even as her healthy figure belies her thin, pale
face. Mary is a study in contrasts and conflicts - she still retains
the charm and innocence of her school days in the convent and
this contrasts with the bitterness and cynicism she often reveals
in her conversation and manner. She loves her husband, but
does not hesitate to hurt him; she defends Jamie before Tyrone
but later admits her own feeling of animosity towards her elder
son.

With the possible exception of Edmund, the mother is the
most completely delineated character in the play. She dominates
every scene even if she is not actually present. All the action
revolves about her -most of the conversations concern her
- just about any kindness or consideration shown in the play
is directed towards the mother. (Even after she is under the
influence of narcotics, she is usually treated with deference.)
And O'Neill has the mother voice many of the ideas and beliefs
he himself had expressed at other times and in other places.

In the first act Mary says that what makes life hard is the
inability to forget; O'Neill, of course, wrote the play so that
he could forgive and forget. Mary uses narcotics to escape the
reality which she despises and return to the past which she
fondly remembers; all the Tyrone men use whiskey to forget
their failings, their lost hopes, or their unfulfilled desires. But if

one cannot forget, one may still "escape" reality by exonerating himself and blaming another.

In the first scene of the second act Mary says no one can help the things life has done to him. If life is responsible (or others) then the individual is relieved of a personal burden of guilt. This idea that life is responsible repeats O'Neill's concern with a Force that shapes or directs mankind. Frederic I. Carpenter commented thus on the problem of responsibility, "Although the four characters of the autobiographical drama seem to wound and to destroy one another by their constant bickerings and conflicts, their true tragedy is caused, rather, by what "life" has done to them - by the unseen forces of their heredity and environment." (See *Eugene O'Neill*, Twayne Publishers, Inc., 1964, p. 24.)

In the second scene of the second act O'Neill continues his commentary on Forces (especially heredity and environment) when he has Mary say that the past is the present and also the future. And a little later she says she has to lie now, especially to herself. This lying to oneself, like the denying of reality through the use of whiskey or narcotics, is part of the attempt to create and maintain a "life-illusion." Throughout the play Mary, like the others, denies the reality which is staring her in the face because it is too painful to accept.

The portrait of the mother is drawn with painstaking care because of her importance to the play and because of O'Neill's great affection for his own mother. Recall that Edmund is sensitive like his mother, looks like his mother, and loves the fog as his mother does. And her gradual withdrawal into herself and away from reality parallels the progress of time in the play - from day into night.

JAMES TYRONE, JR.

Jamie is thirty-four, the ne'er-do-well, elder son who is pampered by his mother and despised by his father. His life has been spent pursuing pleasure in order to escape the pain and mental anguish which he feels but cannot express. His mother and brother defend and sometimes condone what he does and what he fails to do. Physically, mentally, and morally he is a smudged copy of the father - a comparison both would vehemently deny.

Physically, Jamie is built like the father, but he lacks the father's bearing and graceful carriage. Both enjoy their whiskey and both "sowed their wild oats" in their youth. (In the play, Jamie's inordinate attachment to his mother provides still another parallel.) The father is a successful actor; the son could be if he put his mind to it. And when the play ends Jamie and James Tyrone are in a sense left alone together -Mary has "escaped" by taking narcotics; Edmund has "escaped" through the understanding and insight he has gained.

A great part of Jamie's importance to the play stems from the ways in which he contrasts with Edmund, especially regarding attitudes and ideas. Edmund admires and defends Jamie - as noted above both he and the mother make excuses to the father for him. The two brothers share whiskey and women and, as they all mention, Jamie has had a tremendous influence (mostly bad) on his younger brother. But only in the last act does Jamie really become important and then primarily because he "tells" us much about Edmund.

When Jamie tells Edmund that he purposely tried to make a bum out of him in order to make himself look better, we appreciate his candor at the same time as we are dismayed by his revelation. When he then proceeds to blurt out his hatred of Edmund, we again witness the love-hate conflict which each feels. And when O'Neill reveals so much about Jamie, his ideas, and his attitude, he at the same time reveals much about himself.

A number of critics have commented on the animosity which existed among the various members of the family as well as between the two brothers. Frederick I. Carpenter commented thus, "The conflict of older brother with younger - of Cain with Abel, of cynical materialist with aspiring artist - goes far beyond any simple conflict of character. It illuminates the conflicts of two philosophies of life. . . . The conflict between the cynical negation preached by Jamie and the tragic transcendence of these negations." (See *Eugene O'Neill*, Twayne Publishers, 1964, p. 161.)

EDMUND TYRONE

As was noted before, Edmund, the sensitive younger son and the aspiring poet, is supposed to be Eugene O'Neill himself. The choice of the name Edmund is an interesting play on words and ideas. Eugene O'Neill had a younger brother, Edmund, who died some years before Eugene was born; when writing the play Eugene O'Neill takes the name Edmund and then has the mother refer to the son who died some years before as Eugene.

In the last act of the play Edmund (Eugene) tells his father he is a "little in love with death." The question then arises - was O'Neill's substitution of his name for his dead brother's name expressing a death-wish? Or - was O'Neill trying to say that these experiences helped to bring about the "death" of his old self and his subsequent "re-birth" to a new life? (Remember O'Neill said that during his stay in the sanitarium he examined his life - past and future.) Probably the answer to each question is a qualified yes.

Certainly O'Neill was obsessed by the idea of death, pain, and destruction. A number of critics have catalogued the number of deaths, murders, and suicides in his plays. But O'Neill saw death as the ultimate of life - it was not something to be desired or dreaded. In his play Marco Millions he wrote, "Be proud of life! Know in your heart that the living of life can be noble! Be exalted by life! Be inspired by death!" O'Neill wished to have life and have it more abundantly - and for him this was possible if he remained ever conscious of the shadow of death.

During the Day Edmund endures the most, understands the most, and profits the most. He endures the most because he is sensitive to the feelings of others and to his own feelings - although he tries, he cannot figuratively or literally close his eyes to what is happening to all of them. He understands the most because he has studied others as well as himself - through reading and reflection he has learned about himself and others. He profits the most because, as noted earlier, the experiences of this day lead him eventually out of the darkness and into the light - he is able to forgive and forget and thus find the peace of mind which has eluded the others.

During the last act, in the conversation with his father, Edmund speaks of "losing his life" and "finding himself." Having forgotten himself, having put aside greedy fears and hopes and dreams, he says he has found contentment and peace in union with Life - or God. At this point Edmund (O'Neill) becomes both lyrical and mystical in his attempt to find the Reality and the Meaning behind life or mere existence. Lionel Trilling once commented, "Not only has O'Neill tried to encompass more of life than most American writers of his time but almost alone among them he has persistently tried to solve it." (See. "Eugene O'Neill" in the *New Republic* 88 (September 23, 1936), p. 176.)

CATHLEEN

The hired girl Cathleen plays a very small part in the action of the play. Her appearance in Act Three makes possible Mary's discussion of her past for Cathleen's (and the audience's) information. And her comments and attitude provide humorous interludes which relieve the tension. But most important is her actual presence - the fact that she is there and not an O'Neill. Also, some critics think her name is psychologically significant.

As noted earlier, the girl O'Neill married in 1909 and who divorced him in 1912 was named Kathleen. By naming the hired girl Cathleen he reveals, perhaps inadvertently, his concern for what has happened in his personal life. If this is true, we would have to consider his picture of her quite unflattering - ignorant, clumsy, stupid. But if O'Neill wanted to include a Cathleen in order to complete the picture, perhaps the fact that she is not an O'Neill is a back-handed compliment.

Cathleen's presence is important because she is an "outsider" witnessing, participating in, but not understanding what is taking place. She somehow symbolizes those who look but see nothing and listen but hear nothing. Perhaps it is a blessing that one can be so close to tragedy and not realize it. As in Bruegel's *Icarus,* in the face of tragedy, life goes on.

LONG DAY'S JOURNEY INTO NIGHT

CRITICAL COMMENTARY

From the time he first began seriously to write for the theatre, O'Neill had very definite ideas about what he wanted to say and how he wanted to say it. He respected certain critics and he sought certain counsels but he retained his belief in the "rightness" of what he wanted to say and how he wanted to say it. In a letter to George Jean Nathan (a leading literary critic), dated June 20, 1920, O'Neill wrote, "And in this faith I live: That if I have the 'guts' to ignore the megaphone men and what goes with them, to follow the dream and live for that alone, then my real significant bit of truth, and the ability to express it, will be conquered in time ... after the struggle has been long enough and hard enough to merit victory." And throughout his career O'Neill retained this faith in himself and, although he was interested in what the critics and the "megaphone men" had to say, he never wrote merely to please others or to profit himself.

O'Neill has been criticized for being "over-complicated" or "simple-minded"; too "obscure" or "patently apparent." Theater-goers consider his dramas "much ado about nothing" or "too philosophical." But, if his plays at times failed to convey clearly and precisely what he wanted to say, his letters to the newspapers and to his friends did not. In a letter to the *New York Herald Tribune* concerning *The Hairy Ape* (published November 16, 1924) O'Neill wrote, "The subject here is the same ancient one that always was and always will be the subject for drama, and that is man and his struggle with his own fate. The struggle used to be with the gods, but is now with himself, his own past, his attempt to belong." And earlier, in a letter to George Jean Nathan, O'Neill wrote, "The playwright of today must dig at the roots of the sickness of today as he feels it - the death of the old God and the failure of science and materialism to give any satisfactory new one for the surviving primitive religious instinct to find a meaning for life in, and to comfort its fears of death with." Certainly no author could be more specific in outlining what he wanted to do and why he wanted to do it. And yet it is O'Neill's "fate" to continue to be misunderstood.

O'Neill was often criticized for being "morbid," "depressing" and "tragic." In the autobiographical *Long Day's Journey Into Night*, O'Neill, with "tongue in cheek," has the father make the same kind of comment to Edmund Eugene O'Neill's alter ego) about his literary interests: "Where the hell do you get your taste in literature? Filth and despair and pessimism!" For some forty years critics have been asking and attempting to answer the same question. Ironically, it has been O'Neill's writing about this same 'filth and despair and pessimism" that has brought him the most affluent praise and the most adverse criticism.

Few critics and few playgoers are passive about O'Neill and his work - either they consider him "America's greatest playwright" or they dismiss him as a sometimes interesting but really not very important writer. One of the most devastating and derogatory criticisms of O'Neill and his work was written by H. G. Kemelman. In "Eugene O'Neill and the Highbrow Melodrama," he wrote, "to sum up, when a woman walks on stage in an O'Neill melodrama, the chances are ten to one that she is in some way sexually abnormal and if she is, she is certain to be the finest character on the stage." (See *The Bookman*, 75 (September 1932) 486.) And commenting on O'Neill's **diction**, he said, "The **diction** in O'Neill is just as grandiose and extravagant and unreal as the characters who use it." Although Kemelman was the most "cutting" in his commentary, other critics also considered O'Neill to be overly concerned with the "seamier side" of life. Regarding his characters, C. H. Whitman wrote, "His most successful characters are people of rather primitive instincts, misfits, suffering from disease, economic inhibitions, frustrations, from soul-destroying powers which they cannot understand." (See the appendix to *Seven Contemporary Plays*, *Houghton-Mifflin Company*, 1931, p. 555.)

Another critic, S. K. Winther, took O'Neill's concern with "soul-destroying powers" one step further: "It is the very fact that they are tortured by 'soul-destroying powers which they cannot understand' that makes them the embodiment of man's tragic struggle against an unfriendly universe, that gives them universality, that arouses tragic pity, and makes us understand more clearly than we ever understood before just what it means to be human." (See Eugene *O'Neill: A Critical Study*, Random House, 1934, p. 11.) The universality of O'Neill's work certainly contributed to his appeal "to all people and all times." Richard Dana Skinner believed that he had "the poet's gift of reaching to the emotional and moral inwardness of life without any relation to specific events, or times, or people." (See *Eugene O'Neill: A Poet's Quest*, Longmans, Green and Company, 1935, pp. 1-2.) Moreover, Skinner believed that O'Neill's concern with the less attractive part of man's nature contributed to the universality of his work: "He is the poet of the individual soul, of its agony, of its evil will, of its pride, and its lusts, of its rare moments of illumination, of its stumblings and gropings in surrounding darkness, and of its superbly romantic quest for deliverance through loving surrender" (p. 10.)

O'Neill thought of himself as a "bit of a poet" and in a letter to Arthur Hobson Quinn, he wrote, "But where I feel myself most neglected is just where I set most store by myself - as a bit of a poet who has labored with the spoken word to evolve original rhythms of beauty where beauty apparently isn't...." Although O'Neill "labored with the spoken word," he often seemed to have labored in vain. Richard Hayes felt that "O'Neill's insensibility to words-to their lustre and resistance, their shimmer or weightiness -harassed him all his days." (See "Eugene O'Neill: The Tragic Exile," *Theatre Arts,* 47 (October 1963) 68). But for others this shortcoming did not negate the greatness of his vision or the importance of his work. Joseph Wood Krutch made the following comment: "No other playwright has written so much or remained so persistently in the forefront of discussion; no other has devoted himself with such dogged insistence to the single task of writing plays.... At the same time the work of no other contemporary has been more uneven." (See *The American Drama Since 1918, George Braziller, Inc.,* 1957, pp. 77-78.) Many critics felt that O'Neill's work was "uneven," but others felt that even if his literary shortcomings were forgiven, none of his plays could be considered great literature.

Bernard De Voto wrote the following comment following O'Neill's selection for the Nobel Prize in Literature, "Nowhere do we encounter the finality or the reconciliation of great art, nowhere is any fragment of human life remade for us in understanding and splendor. What he tells us is simple, familiar, superficial, and even trite - and because of a shallow misunderstanding of Freud and windy mysticism, sometimes flatly wrong." (See "Minority Report," *Saturday Review* 15 (November 21, 1936) 16). In his *Trends in 20th Century Drama,*

Frederick Lumley commented, "He had an outstanding sense of theatre and could write a good play; but he was not a genius and never wrote a masterpiece." *(Barrie and Rockliff* - London, 1960, p. 135). Eric Bentley also commented on the shortcomings of O'Neill in his essay, "Trying to like O'Neill," but he concluded by saying, "If one does not like O'Neill, it is not really he that one dislikes: it is our age-of which like the rest of us he is more the victim than the master." (See *In Search of Theatre, Alfred A. Knopf, Inc.,* 1952, p. 234.) But for every detractor, O'Neill has had a half-dozen ardent admirers.

Sinclair Lewis in his 1930 Nobel Prize for Literature acceptance speech alluded to the genius of O'Neill and his worthiness to receive this Prize (which he did two years later). He credited O'Neill with utterly transforming the American drama in ten or twelve years. George Jean Nathan declared that "O'Neill is the foremost dramatist in the American theatre because no one has anything like his ability to delve into and appraise character, his depth of knowledge of his fellow men, his sweep and pulse of high resolve, his command of a theatre and its manifold workings." And commenting on *Long Day's Journey Into Night* in the *New York Herald Tribune*, Lewis Gannett wrote, "No play Eugene O'Neill ever wrote speaks more eloquently.... Certainly on one, henceforth, will write of his other plays without remembering this, the most revealing of himself."

THE CRITICS AND LONG DAY'S JOURNEY INTO NIGHT

Because of the autobiographical nature of the play, critics have been more concerned with commenting on the significance of particular passages, explaining particular allusions, and offering varied and often conflicting explanations than with attempting to evaluate the dramatic worth of *Long Day's Journey Into Night.* They call it interesting, thought-provoking, revealing, soul-searching, but they seem to feel that any real criticism of the play is unwarranted and unworthy. (Ironically the critics seem to have more respect for Eugene O'Neill now that he is dead than they ever had while he was alive.) The rather non-committal comments below illustrate the apparent "hands-off policy" regarding the play.

Harold Clurman in his commentary on *Long Day's Journey* repeats many of the comments previously made about O'Neill and his writing ability. He speaks of this play as being a "painfully autobiographical work" and then adds, "The accusation of his own guilt and obsessive desire to purge himself of it through blame nags him; hence the repetitiousness of phrases and scenes; it is a planned repetitiousness, often wearisome to the reader (or the spectator) but organic to the author." (See "Theatre," *Nation,* 183 (November 24, 1956) 466.) Mr. Clurman seems to "beg the question" of whether or not the play is "great" or even "good."

One of the most succinct commentaries on O'Neill and his plays was written by Frederic I. Carpenter. He makes a number of perceptive comments, but when he attempts to deal with *Long Day's Journey* he appears hesitant. He too stresses the autobiographical elements: *"Long Day's Journey* describes the mid-world of middle class family life, and its greatness lies in its simple domestication both of tragic emotion and of human insight." (See *Eugene O'Neill,* Twayne Publishers, Inc., 1964, p. 159.) Another commentator who evaluated the play in terms of the lives it portrayed was Peter Bugel: "The greatness of the play is that it succeeds where they failed in granting atonement for all their real and imagined grievances." (See "The O'Neill's: A Tragic Epilogue to the Drama," *53 Life* (October 26, 1962) 70B.)

In probably one of the finest and most perceptive reviews written by John Chapman, he tells why he thinks *Long Day's Journey* is a magnificent and beautiful play. He dismisses the autobiographical element by saying it could have been written about anybody else. He calls the play "one of the great dramas of any time" and calls attention to the "profound compassion of the writing" and the "great depths of his [O'Neill's] sympathy." He continues, "As they tell of themselves, each in a long monologue, these people become larger, than their own small lives; they become humanity, looking for something but not knowing exactly what it is looking for." (See *New York Daily News*, November 8, 1956).

Walter Kerr's commentary begins with a review of the autobiographical elements and ends by calling the play an "obligation" for anyone who cares about the American theater. In between he raises doubts about whether *Long Day's Journey* is really a play and discusses points at which the melodramatic almost supersedes the dramatic. But his final comment is an affirmation of O'Neill's genius and the play's greatness: "It is a stunning theatrical experience." (See *New York Herald Tribune*, November 8, 1956).

A number of critics felt that in this play O'Neill reverted to the **realism** which was his forte in the early plays. Henry Hewes commented that ". . . there is a breadth to *Long Day's Journey Into Night* that may make it the most universal piece of stage **realism** ever turned out by an American playwright. For doesn't it expose the forces that work both to unite and tear asunder all human groups?" (See "O'Neill: 100 proof - Not a Blend," *Saturday Review*, 39 November 24, 1956) 30.)

Note that Hewes refers to "forces" at the same time that he speaks of "stage realism." For O'Neill the forces were real.

In a letter to Lawrence Langner, dated August 11, 1940, O'Neill made an observation that might well be applied to *Long Day's Journey Into Night*. Concerning *The Iceman Cometh*, O'Neill wrote; "What I mean is, there are moments in it that suddenly strip the secret soul of a man stark naked, not in cruelty or moral superiority, but with an understanding compassion which sees him as a victim of the ironies of life and of himself. Those moments are for me the depth of tragedy, with nothing more that can possible be said." Certainly, it was his ability to "strip the secret soul of a man stark naked" that has assured O'Neill's reputation as one of the most outstanding and influential dramatists of all time. Brooks Atkinson concluded his review of *Long Day's Journey Into Night* with these words: "*Long Day's Journey Into Night* has been worth waiting for. It restores the drama to literature and the theatre to art." (See *New York Times*, November 8, 1956.)

Where O'Neill will rank in the final analysis is difficult to say. But any criticism of O'Neill and his work should be predicated on the critic's or commentator's understanding of and respect for two of O'Neill's beliefs:

1. "A play is written to be expressed through the theatre, and only on its merits in a theatre can a final judgment be passed on it with justice."

2. "Truth, in the theatre as in life, is eternally difficult, just as the easy is the everlasting lie."

LONG DAY'S JOURNEY INTO NIGHT

ESSAY QUESTIONS AND ANSWERS

Question: What did O'Neill believe should be the playwright's purpose in writing?

Answer: In a letter to George Jean Nathan, O'Neill expressed what he believed to be the most important concern for any modern-day writer: "The playwright of today must dig at the roots of the sickness of today as he feels it - the death of the old God and the failure of science and materialism to give any satisfactory new one for the surviving primitive religious instinct to find a meaning for life in, and to comfort the fears of death with. It seems to me that anyone trying to do big work nowadays must have this big subject behind all the little subjects of his plays or novels, or he is scribbling around the surface of things." (Quoted in Joseph Wood Krutch, *The American Drama Since 1918*, Random House, 1939, pp. 192-193.) Certainly O'Neill, more than any other writer, has tried to "dig at the roots," although many resent his "digging in the dirt."

At another time he wrote that he was convinced that "the only subject worth writing about" is "man's glorious, self-destructive struggle to make the Force express him" - O'Neill believed this

Force could be God, fate, or heredity. Both quotations show his concern with life and the meaning of life - and this was his purpose in writing.

Question: Why are most of O'Neill's plays termed "autobiographical"?

Answer: O'Neill's first plays deal primarily with the sea and reflected and referred to many of his own experiences as a sailor. His later plays, by his own admission, contained characters and recalled situations from his own life. And very early in his career O'Neill noted his concern with "our biological past creating our present," which would indicate his own awareness of the influence which his family and his own experiences had upon him and his work. But it was the publication of his autobiographical *Long Day's Journey Into Night* which sent the critics and the commentators scurrying to the stories of his life. Certainly, as O'Neill was the first to admit, his "biological past" created his present" and helped to create his plays, but to attempt to pin-point every character, every **allusion**, every setting, every occurrence, is to negate the importance of O'Neill's creative genius.

Question: Why has O'Neill's popularity fluctuated over the years?

Answer: The fluctuations in O'Neill's career are as much the result of the unevenness of his work and his unwillingness to "compromise" his convictions as they are of the vagaries of the critics and the theatre-going public. Volumes have been written on the unevenness of his work and it is a foregone conclusion that O'Neill had more genius than talent - too often his aim exceeded his grasp. But from the very beginning he maintained that he would not be influenced by the "megaphone men" and he did not care what the critics and ordinary theatre-goers thought; he once commented that he wrote for the minority and that his plays "will live for them. So what the Hell!" The majority of thoughtful critics (and theater-goers) have appreciated O'Neill and his work, but it would be difficult to label him a "popular" dramatist because of the harshness of the reality he presented. In commenting on a recent revival of interest in and appreciation of O'Neill, Joseph Wood Krutch wrote, "O'Neill's plays owe some of their present popularity to the fact that, by comparison with many others more recent, they are cheerful." (See "Why the O'Neill Star is Rising," *The New York Times Magazine*, March 19, 1961. p. 111.)

Question: Why did O'Neill choose August, 1912, for the time when the action takes place?

Answer: The summer of 1912 was most significant for O'Neill. He had been to college and flunked out, had been unable to hold a job, had married and been divorced, had spent several years as a common seaman, had "bummed around" New York, and was now, for the first time practically, doing something that he liked - writing. It was in 1912 that O'Neill discovered he had tuberculosis, and it was during his confinement in a sanitarium that he reviewed his life and decided he wanted to be a writer. Certainly when he decided to write an "autobiographical drama" O'Neill wished to select a particular time span that was most significant to his development as a writer and a person - and this time was August 1912.

Question: Discuss briefly some of the apparent autobiographical elements in the play.

Answer: Most of the names, places, events, and characterizations in this play are taken directly from Eugene O'Neill's life. The author substituted his name for the name of a younger brother (Edmund) who had died many years before. James and Jamie were the names of his father and brother. And his mother's first name was Mary although for many years she used her middle name. In the play the stingy father, the dissolute brother, the dope-addicted mother, and the sensitive younger son in many ways parallel the O'Neill family. And the setting - the living room of their summer home - is a near replica of the one in the old family home in New London, Conn.

Probably the most interesting and in many ways the most surprising are the number of incidents related on stage which are taken directly from the known facts about the O'Neill family. To name but a few - the father's acting career, Jamie's carousing, Eugene's flunking college and going to sea, the mother's piano playing. Even the story about Shaughnessy is partially authentic. About the only thing O'Neill omitted was any reference to his marriage - but perhaps his naming of the hired girl was his acknowledgment of this episode.

Question: Discuss the most significant elements of O'Neill's stage setting for this play.

Answer: Basically the stage setting consists of a somewhat shabby living room furnished in the style of the early 1900s. But three elements of the set are given prominence and can contribute much to one's understanding and appreciation of the action that is to take place in this setting - the two double doorways at the rear, the two bookcases, and the overhead chandelier. One doorway leads into a dark back parlor and almost all entrances are made from this room; thus symbolically and actually the characters move from darkness into light. The other doorway leads into the front parlor which is rarely used; because the mother goes into this room when she has lost contact with reality, the room seems to symbolize escape or freedom. The two bookcases are referred to at a number of points in the play because one contains Edmund's books and the other contains Tyrone's, and the books which each read reflect their respective interests. The turning on and off of the bulbs in the chandelier during the last act matches the revelations which each member of the family makes about himself - and provides another opportunity for comments about Tyrone's stinginess.

Question: Discuss briefly O'Neill's references to fog in this play.

Answer: The fog is used to set the scene since the house is located near the harbor. But more important is the use of fog to symbolize and at the same time parallel the family's attempt to obscure reality. When the play opens, the fog has cleared although reference is made to the foghorns which sounded during the previous night. By noon, a haze indicates that the fog is coming back. By nightfall the fog has returned and the foghorns and ships' bells are again heard. When the play opens, the other members of the family think that the mother has been cured of her drug addiction, by noon they suspect her, and by nightfall they are convinced that she will never be cured. All of them, including the mother, attempted to obscure and deny reality - the fog also obscures reality.

The fog is used also by O'Neill (in the person of Edmund) not to symbolize a way to escape reality but to symbolize the inability of man to see beyond what is "apparently" reality. When Edmund tells the father that in the past for a very few moments he had been able to escape from himself and thus belong to Life itself, he speaks of his existence before and after these **episodes** as being one of the "fog people" - one who attempts to understand and explain the mystery of life.

Question: Why is James Tyrone's stinginess emphasized so much throughout the play?

Answer: O'Neill's over-riding concern with portraying James Tyrone as a stingy man who was more concerned with accumulating wealth than with providing adequately for his family is interpreted by many to be the author's indictment of his own father and an accurate portrayal of his penuriousness. Although he was a wealthy man, James O'Neill, Sr., was inclined to be cautious and saving, probably because of his impoverished youth. But the many references to Tyrone's stinginess in this play are more important as a unifying **theme** and a symbolic manifestation of the family's inherent selfishness. By emphasizing the father's stinginess, each member of the family is given an opportunity to blame him for what they are. They all need someone or something for a scapegoat.

Question: Discuss briefly Mary's comment, "The past is the present, isn't it? It's the future too."

Answer: O'Neill was always concerned with the forces (Fate, heredity) that shape men's lives. What happened in the past does influence the present and the future. What we have done or what we have failed to do often returns to haunt us. So it is with Mary Tyrone and so it is with the others - all are hunted by the specter of what "might-have-been." James said he could have been as great an actor as Booth, if he had not tied himself to a single money-making play; Mary says she would have never have become an addict if she hadn't married James and borne Edmund; Jamie says he might have been able to overcome his problems if the mother had not become addicted again; and Edmund (O'Neill) - perhaps the pain, suffering, dope-addiction, drunkenness, and immorality helped to mold him into the great dramatist which he was to become.

Question: Some critics felt the many quotations O'Neill used in the last act were unnecessary and contributed little to the play. How would you "justify" O'Neill's use of these quotations?

Answer: O'Neill selected passages from authors and works that expressed what he wanted to say better than he could. Each of the passages refers to some question he had pondered, some idea he had accepted; or some emotion he had felt. A quick look at some of the passages will indicate their particular significance:

They are not long, the weeping and the laughter, Love and desire and hate: (Dowson)

O'Neill tries to say the same thing when he tells the father about the few times he was able to find real peace and contentment.

We are such as dreams are made on. . . . (Shakespeare)

By substituting manure for dreams he not only indicates that man is unable to escape reality, but also expresses his disillusionment with mankind.

If you would not feel the horrible burden of Time weighing on your shoulders and crushing you to the earth, be drunken continually. (Baudelaire)

Again he expresses his concern with escaping reality.

The dead are dancing with the dead, The dust is whirling with the dust. (Wilde)

This expresses O'Neill's view of his family because they are unable or unwilling to face life and live it.

There is no help, for all these things are so, And all the world is bitter as a tear. (Swinburne)

Could any passage better express O'Neill's state of mind at this point in his life?

BIBLIOGRAPHY

BOOK

Alexander, Doris. *The Tempering of Eugene O'Neill*. New York: Hartcourt, Brace and World, Inc., 1962.

[Comprehensive view of O'Neill's early years - ends with the death of James O'Neill, Sr. in 1920.]

Boulton, Agnes. *Part of a Long Story*. Garden City, New York: Doubleday and Company, 1958.

[Mostly chit-chat about the first few years of her marriage to O'Neill.]

Browen, Croswell. *The Curse of the Misbegotten*. New York: McGraw-Hill, 1959.

[Written with the assistance of Shane O'Neill; well-documented and surprisingly unbiased.]

Brown, John Mason. *Dramatis Personae.* New York: Viking Press, 1963.

[Includes this noted reviewer's perceptive commentary and criticism of a number of O'Neill's plays.]

Carpenter, Frederic I. *Eugene O'Neill.* New York: Twayne Publishers, 1964.

[Relates O'Neill's life to his plays - a good quick review of the man and his work.]

Clark, Barrett H. *Eugene O'Neill: The Man and his New York:* New York: McBride and Company, 1929.

[One of the earliest books on O'Neill - interesting review of his life and early work.]

Deutsch, Helen and Stella Hanau. *The Provincetown - A Story of the Theatre.* New York: Farrar and Rinehart, 1931.

[An interesting account of the theatre group which greatly influenced O'Neill and vice-versa.]

Dusenbury, Winifred L. *The **Theme** of Loneliness in Modern American Drama.* Gainesville: University of Florida Press, 1960.

[Makes a number of perceptive comments about O'Neill when using his plays to develop her thesis.]

Engel, Edwin. *The Haunted Heroes of Eugene O'Neill.* Cambridge: Harvard University Press, 1953.

[Interesting detailed analysis of major plays and major themes.]

Engel, Edwin A. "Ideas in the Plays of Eugene O'Neill," in *Ideas in the Drama* edited by John Gassner. New York: Columbia University Press, 1964.

[Sees O'Neill's adolescence as the "source of all nourishment and emotional and intellectual."]

Falk, Doris V. *Eugene O'Neill and the Tragic Tension.* Brunswick, New Jersey: Rutgers University Press, 1958.

[Excellent study of O'Neill's plays - many good points and very readable.]

Gagey, Edmond M. *"Eugene O'Neill" in Revolution in American Drama.* New York: Columbia University Press, 1947.

[Brief review of each major play plus a list of O'Neill's important contributions to the theatre.]

Gelb, Arthur and Barbara. *O'Neill.* New York: Harper and Brothers, 1960.

[Most comprehensive work on O'Neill to date - very worthwhile and readable.]

Krutch, Joseph Wood. *The American Drama since 1918.* New York: Random House, 1939.

[Contains an interesting chapter on tragedy which centers on O'Neill.]

Langner, Lawrence. *The Magic Curtain.* New York: E. P. Dutton and Company, 1951.

[This life of Langner contains several chapters on O'Neill and the texts of several of his letters.]

Nathan, George Jean. *The Magic Mirror.* New York: Alfred A. Knopf, 1960.

[Contains several interesting and important essays on O'Neill.]

Parks, Edd Winfield. *Segments of Southern Thought.* Athens: University of Georgia Press, 1938.

[Contains an essay on O'Neill's use of symbolism.]

Quinn, A. H. A. *History of the American Drama from the Civil War to the Present Day.* 2. Volumes. New York: Crofts, 1945.

[Interesting section on O'Neill discusses his poetic and mystical qualities.]

Simonson, Lee. *The Stage is Set.* New York: Harcourt, Brace, 1932.

[Many perceptive comments on O'Neill sprinkled throughout the book.]

Skinner, Richard Dana. *Eugene O'Neill: A Poet's Quest.* New York: Longmans, Green and Company, 1935.

[Well-written, perceptive, valuable study of the "inner continuity" of O'Neill's plays.]

Straumann, Heinrich. *American Literature in the Twentieth Century.* London: Hutchinson's University Library, 1951.

[Very brief but very interesting commentary on O'Neill included.]

Winther, Sophus Keith. *Eugene O'Neill: A Critical Study.* New York: Random House, 1934.

[An early study showing considerable insight into the man and his work.]

PERIODICALS

Alexander, Doris M. "Eugene O'Neill as Social Critic," *American Quarterly*, 6 (Winter 1954) 349-363.

[An extended analysis of O'Neill's criticism of modern society.]

Bentley, Eric. "Trying to Like O'Neill," *Kenyon Review,* 14 (July 1952) 476-492.

[A witty, very perceptive article which is widely quoted.]

Brown, John Mason. "Dat Ole Davil and a Hard God," *Saturday Review of Literature*, 35 (February 16, 1952) 32-34.

[Review of *Anna Christie* and *Desire Under the Elms* - contains many interesting comments and comparisons.]

Clark, Barrett H. "Aeschylus and O'Neill," *The English Journal*, XXI, No. 9 (November 1932) 701-705.

[Discusses O'Neill's use of elements of the Greek drama to express problems of modern life.]

Clurman, Harold. "At Odds with Gentility," *Nation,* 194 (April 7, 1962) 312.

[Review of two studies concerning O'Neill - a number of interesting comments.]

De Voto, Bernard. "Minority Report," *Saturday Review,* 15 (November 21, 1936) 3.

[Sharply critical of O'Neill's selection for the Nobel Prize in literature.]

Eaton, Walter Pritchard. "O'Neill: New Risen Attic Stream?" *American Scholar,* 6 (Summer 1937) 304-312.

[Valuable commentary on the Greek tradition as seen in *Desire Under the Elms.*]

Fagin, N. Bryllion. "Eugene O'Neill." *Antioch Review,* 14 (March 1954) 14-26.

[An evaluation of O'Neill published shortly after his death.]

Granger, Bruce J. "Illusion and Reality in Eugene O'Neill," *Modern Language Notes*, 73 (March 1958) 179-186.

[See O'Neill's plays as portraying the dilemma of modern man.]

Hayes, Richard. "Eugene O'Neill: The Tragic in Exile," *Theatre Arts*, 47 (October 1963) 16-17.

[Discussion of O'Neill and his insensibility to words.]

Kemelman, H. G., "Eugene O'Neill and the Highbrow Melodrama," *Bookman,* 75 (September 1932) 482-491.

[A vehement attack on O'Neill and his work which portrays him as a kind of fraud.]

Krutch, Joseph Wood. "Eugene O'Neill, the Lonely Revolutionary," *Theatre Arts,* 36 (April 1952) 29-30.

[Krutch's comments are, as always, pithy and pertinent.]

Krutch, Joseph Wood. "O'Neill's Tragic Sense," *American Scholar,* 16 (Summer 1947) 283-290.

[Discusses difficulty of evaluating O'Neill - concludes he has genius but lacks talent.]

Krutch, Joseph Wood. "Why the O'Neill Star is Rising." *The New York Times Magazine*, (March 19, 1961) 36-37.

[Discusses O'Neill's significance and worth for a new generation.]

Mullett, Mary B. "The Extraordinary Story of Eugene O'Neill," *American Magazine*, 94 (November 1922) 34.

[After forty years, still one of the best portraits of O'Neill ever presented - widely quoted.]

Parks, Edd Winfield. "Eugene O'Neill's Symbolism," *Sewanee Review*, 43 (October-December 1935) 436-450.

[Attempt to explain O'Neill's symbols and philosophy.]

Peck, Seymour. "Talk with Mrs. O'Neill," *New York Times*, 4 (November 1956) 11, 1.6.

Carlotta Monterey describes the background of *Long Day's Journey* - other interesting comments.]

Stamm, Rudolph. "The Dramatic Experiments of Eugene O'Neill," *English Studies*, 28 (February 1947) 1-15.

[Surveys the main phases of O'Neill's experimentation and development.]

Trilling, Lionel. "Eugene O'Neill," *The New Republic*, 88 (September 23, 1936) 176-179.

[Perceptive discussion of O'Neill's philosophy of life as expressed in his plays.]

Whitman, Robert F., "O'Neill's Search for a Language of the Theatre," *Quarterly Journal of Speech*, XVI, No. 2 (April 1960) 326-332.

[Brief review of O'Neill's many and varied manners of speech: realism, expressionism, symbolism, fantasy, poetry.]

Winther, Sophus Keith. "*Desire Under the Elms:* A Modern Tragedy," *Modern Drama*, 3 (December 1960) 326-332.

[Discussion of the tragedy of modern life in the idiom of ancient Greece.]

Young, Stark. "Eugene O'Neill: Notes from a Critic's Diary." *Harper,* 214 (June 1957) 66-71.

[Interesting, candid article by a personal friend.]

COLLECTIONS OF CRITICAL ARTICLES AND ESSAYS

Cargill, Oscar and others. *O'Neill and His Plays - Four Decades of Criticism.* New York: New York University Press, 1961.

Gassner, John. *O'Neill: A collection of Critical Essays.* Engle wood Cliffs, New Jersey: Prentice-Hall, Inc., 1964.

Miller, Jordan Y. *Playwright's Progress: O'Neill and the Critics.* Fair Lawn, New Jersey: Scott, Foreman and Company, 1965.

.

Milton Keynes UK
Ingram Content Group UK Ltd.
UKHW020859110624
443837UK00013B/368